Praise for *Math Workshop*...

Math Workshop is our school's primary resource for providing *all* students with an opportunity to access mathematical concepts and skills. It helps teachers and students see that math can be fun. It helps build student resilience and confidence in mathematics. And it promotes differentiated instruction, student discourse, and strategy sharing. Look no further than *Math Workshop!*

—Jason Pannutti, principal, Bren Mar Park Elementary School,
   Alexandria, Virginia

Regardless of the curriculum you use, *Math Workshop* creates a clear vision of how math classrooms can be a space for engaging all children. By using the math workshop model, students' learning is differentiated, students have the opportunity to work with their teacher in small groups, students are provided choice in how they spend their time, and students do math centered around big ideas. So many resources exist related to reading and writing workshop models—I'm excited that there is now one for math!

—Lucy Kersting, math coach, Clark County School District, Las Vegas, Nevada

Math Workshop drives explicit and differentiated math instruction for all students. The resource clearly lays out five steps for implementing math workshop. The "look-fors" included as reproducibles are easy to follow a a great resource for administrators to use during walk-throughs and teach observations.

—Amber K. Walters, principal, Nora Elementary School, Indianapolis, Indiana

Math Workshop expertly blends workshop philosophy with practical ideas, strategies, and structures to engage *all* students in high-quality mathematics learning experiences. The resource brings together all of the components of math workshop and is supported by research-based best practices. Jennifer Lempp's mantra, "Go Slow to Go Fast!" stays with teachers as they develop structures, routines, and a community of mathematicians. The video clips and reflection questions provide powerful guidance as teachers implement and refine their math workshop practices. It feels like Jennifer is there, coaching teachers as they read, plan, teach, and reflect. This is an essential, "go-to" resource for all teachers of mathematics, coaches, and administrators.

—Melissa Pearson, Supervisor of Mathematics, K–5, West Windsor-Plainsboro
   Regional School District, West Windsor Township, New Jersey

Math Workshop is an incredible resource for educators who want to build their understanding of the what, why, and how of developing an effective math workshop. It has everything teachers might need to develop and improve the structure of their math block, including sample minilessons, number sense routines, and video clips showing math workshop in action!

—Lindsey Covey, math instructional coach, Title 1 School, Falls Church, Virginia

Educators today face daunting challenges in their classrooms—how do we meet the diverse needs of our students so that they can all achieve at high levels? This challenge can feel even more overwhelming in the mathematics classroom. In *Math Workshop*, Jennifer Lempp effectively makes the case for successfully implementing a workshop structure that meets the needs of all young mathematicians. Once you've experienced the innumerable benefits of math workshop, you'll never want to go back to your old methods of instruction—and your students will be *begging* for more math!

—Katie Eustis, fifth-grade teacher, Woodley Hills Elementary School, Fairfax County, Virginia

Math Workshop is a pedagogical philosophy that transcends curriculum. It enhances student agency by making learning more student-centered—pushing students to reflect, reason, collaborate, communicate, and make sense of mathematical content—transforming them from math students to student mathematicians. Jennifer Lempp details in clear, manageable, immediately actionable steps how every teacher—novice to seasoned—can elevate core mathematics instruction to simultaneously provide intervention and enrichment, thereby improving student achievement and engagement. Working through this book is like welcoming Jennifer as your personal instructional coach. Her strategies are practical and her tone is encouraging because she's been there. As educators, we want to implement the math workshop model in its entirety immediately; however, Jennifer helps us take comfort in knowing that this is a journey best navigated one step at a time.

—Trish Kepler, math coordinator, The Greenwich Country Day School, Greenwich, Connecticut

This resource is the perfect companion text for our district course for teachers who are seeking to implement math workshop. The included structures and components enable teachers to meet students' individual learning needs while empowering students to be more self-directed. As teachers promote collaboration, problem solving, and communication throughout their learner-driven classrooms, *Math Workshop* helps them take their instructional practice to the next level.

—Sarah Putnam, Director of Teaching and Learning, Arlington Public Schools, Arlington, Virginia

Math Workshop

Five Steps to Implementing Guided Math, Learning Stations, Reflection, and More

Jennifer Lempp

FOREWORD BY SHERRY PARRISH

 GRADES K–5
With Video Streaming

Math Solutions
Sausalito, California, USA

Math Solutions
One Harbor Drive, Suite 101
Sausalito, California USA 94965
www.mathsolutions.com

Library of Congress Cataloging-in-Publication Data
Names: Lempp, Jennifer, author.
Title: Math workshop : five steps to implementing guided math, learning stations, reflection, and more, grades K-5 / Jennifer Lempp ; foreword by Sherry Parrish.
Other titles: Five steps to implementing guided math, learning stations, reflection, and more, grades K-5
Description: Sausalito, California, USA : Math Solutions, [2017] | Includes bibliographical references.
Identifiers: LCCN 2017040495| ISBN 9781935099611 (pbk.) | ISBN 1935099612
Subjects: LCSH: Mathematics--Study and teaching (Elementary)-—United States.
Classification: LCC QA135.6 .L445 2017 | DDC 372.7/044—dc23
LC record available at https://lccn.loc.gov/2017040495

ISBN-13: 978-1-935099-61-1
ISBN-10: 1-935099-61-2

Math Solutions is a division of Houghton Mifflin Harcourt.

MATH SOLUTIONS® and associated logos are trademarks or registered trademarks of Houghton Mifflin Harcourt Publishing Company. Other company names, brand names, and product names are the property and/or trademarks of their respective owners.

Executive Editor: Jamie Ann Cross
Production Manager: Denise A. Botelho
Cover design: Wanda Espana, Wee Design Group
Cover photo: (front cover image) Topic Images, Inc. / (classroom stills) Friday's Films / (author photo) Abigail Bobo Photography
Photo credits: pp. 153–154, ©Photodisc/Getty Images
Interior design and composition: Publishers' Design and Production Services, Inc.

Printed in the United States of America.

3 4 5 6 7 8 9 10 11 0304 26 25 24 23 22 21 20 19 18
4510005225   ABCDE

A Message from Math Solutions

We at Math Solutions believe that teaching math well calls for increasing our understanding of the math we teach, seeking deeper insights into how students learn mathematics, and refining our lessons to best promote students' learning.

Math Solutions shares classroom-tested lessons and teaching expertise from our faculty of professional learning consultants as well as from other respected math educators. Our publications are part of the nationwide effort we've made since 1984 that now includes

- more than five hundred face-to-face professional development programs each year for teachers and administrators in districts across the country;
- professional development books that span all math topics taught in kindergarten through high school;
- videos for teachers and for parents that show math lessons taught in actual classrooms;
- on-site visits to schools to help refine teaching strategies and assess student learning; and
- free online support, including grade-level lessons, book reviews, inservice information, and district feedback.

For information about all of the products and services we have available, please visit our website at www.mathsolutions.com. You can also contact us to discuss math professional learning needs by calling (800) 868-9092 or by sending an email to info@mathsolutions.com.

We're always eager for your feedback and interested in learning about your particular needs. We look forward to hearing from you.

Math Solutions.
FOUNDED BY MARILYN BURNS

To my three favorite little mathematicians,
my children—Mason, Claire, and Sophia.

I hope you always see the beauty of learning
and the joy in numbers.

Brief Contents

(continued)

Contents

(continued)

(continued)

(continued)

(continued)

Reproducibles

All reproducibles are available as downloadable, printable versions at www.mathsolutions.com/mathworkshopreproducibles.

Foreword

Have you ever met someone and believed you were destined to connect? When I first met Jennifer Lempp, I knew we were kindred math spirits with intertwining pedagogical beliefs about what it means to teach and learn mathematics with understanding. Her vision and passion for student learning through math workshop inspired me, and I knew her expertise with elementary and middle school classrooms in this critical area would be a gift for us all.

Math Workshop addresses the question asked by every mathematics teacher, "How do I engage, challenge, and support the needs of *all* learners in my classroom?" Jennifer successfully tackles this difficult question through the math workshop model, a philosophy that incorporates accessible tasks, open-ended problem solving, individual and small-group guided instruction, student choice, and content immersed in the big ideas in mathematics. This comprehensive resource masterfully unlocks the essential characteristics of math workshop with a resonating theme of students as "doers" of mathematics and teachers as facilitators.

> *Math Workshop* addresses the question asked by every mathematics teacher, "How do I engage, challenge, and support the needs of *all* learners in my classroom?"

Whether you are new to math workshop or looking for a more effective way to implement this learning platform, *Math Workshop* provides a step-by-step approach to building a classroom environment intentionally organized to support *all* students in developing and understanding mathematics. The "who, what, when, where, and why" of math workshop are expertly addressed in a clear, easy-to-follow layout. From suggestions for the physical arrangement of your classroom to choosing rich tasks, every detail is discussed to support you in a seamless implementation of the math workshop model.

Lempp's personal experiences using math workshop are invaluable to the reader. She knows the essential foundations needed to establish this structure as a cornerstone of the mathematics classroom. The resource guides us through the characteristics of math workshop using a perfect balance of research and personal application to develop seven core tenets: students as doers of mathematics, the role of student choice, classroom discourse, student collaboration, productive struggle through rich tasks, the teacher as a facilitator, and the importance of working with individual and/or small groups of students. Throughout the resource, Lempp encourages readers to "go slow to go fast." She urges us to take time to test ideas, try different math workshop structures, and revisit ideas until our students and we are comfortable.

Lempp expertly leads us through her masterpiece, making sure we are prepared to take steps in our own classrooms. "Twenty Days to a Classroom Culture That Works" (Chapter 2) targets foundational ideas of math workshop and offers practical suggestions for classroom arrangements to provide physical space for guided math groups, learning stations, and whole-group discussions. Twenty minilessons (plenty for the first month of school) are also included to establish norms for a safe mathematics learning community and to support students in understanding routines and procedures used during math workshop.

Classroom videos are incorporated throughout this resource to provide invaluable support in building our understanding of math workshop as well as offering a vehicle for formative assessment through the lenses of the featured classrooms. Seeing math workshop in action offers us in-the-moment opportunities to observe minilessons, small-group discussions and tasks, learning stations, whole-group processing, and the many flexible structures used in math workshop.

Math Workshop embraces a teaching and learning philosophy that works for all students, all classrooms, all teachers, and all curricula. The flexibility in its structure supports both teachers and students and keeps the mathematics classroom engaging, fresh, and purposeful. If you are interested in building mathematicians and immersing students in "just-right" mathematics that moves beyond a "one-size-fits-all" approach, then you have found the right resource. *Math Workshop* is your game changer!

—Sherry Parrish, author of *Number Talks: Whole Number Computation* and coauthor of *Number Talks: Fractions, Decimals, and Percentages*

Acknowledgments

I first and foremost acknowledge the many students who inspire me every day with their brilliance. I wish all students could see themselves as I see them—full of limitless potential! Because of them, I am continually on the lookout for ways to make their hours in school more rewarding, engaging, and enjoyable. They push me to be a better teacher and to think differently about teaching mathematics. The ideas in *Math Workshop* emerged because of them. So, really, this book is a product of each of my students. I'll never forget that or any of them.

I also couldn't have written this book without the influence of the amazing administrators and teachers I have met over the years. I feel privileged to work with dedicated and talented colleagues, and I've learned so much from all of you. The world is a better place because of your passion, hard work, determination, and love of children. Special acknowledgments to Matt Wight, Debbie Lane, and Maureen Boland—you challenged me and saw things in me that I didn't realize existed. Your leadership and your willingness to support my growth allowed me to think outside the box. And a special shout-out to the teachers at Rolling Valley Elementary—Emily Griswold, Breanna Wallace Tucker, Shannon Robinson, Ashleigh Long, Fiona McGonigal, Merrie Joy Hrabak, and Chrissy Callaway—you enthusiastically and openly shared your classrooms with me for the purpose of *Math Workshop*.

I couldn't have authored *Math Workshop* without the brainpower of my friends and informal editors who read many of my drafts and offered feedback. Erica Riley and Casey Reeves, this book started before I even knew you, but now I can't imagine its existence without you.

The people at Math Solutions are my superheroes! Patty Clark, your kind words and encouragement to present *Math Workshop* to others has meant the world to me. Mary Mitchell, I don't know how you put up with me— you saw the good in my drafts and helped make the content worth reading. From responding to my late-night texts to answering my panicked emails, you never flinched. You were always the calm in my stormy chapters. Denise Botelho, you made magic happen! Your vision for making my marked-up manuscript look like a work of art, your patience with me as I navigated the publishing world, and your responsiveness to my requests for help are so appreciated. To my editor, Jamie Cross, your smile and positivity have been appreciated from the beginning. You told me to believe that this book would happen, and because those words came from you, I believed. I always knew that my work would be in good hands with your expertise and vision. The four of you believed in my message and provided the encouragement, flexibility, and support I needed over the last several years while my messy pages and random thoughts were crafted into a cohesive book. I also want to thank Perry Pickert and his team at Friday's Films for filming the beauty that I see when I observe students doing math workshop. You captured the excitement and wonder as well as the mathematical reasoning that happens in classrooms.

Most of all, I thank my family. My wonderful children, Mason, Claire, and Sophia—you saw me at my laptop way more hours than I had hoped. I'll never forget you saying, "You are such a hard worker, Mommy!" Those words got me through the toughest chapters to write, though the "mom guilt" was heavy. I know having an educator for a mother isn't always easy. I'm looking for the learning opportunity in everything and constantly trying to do math with you (because I find such joy in seeing the amazing mathematician in each of you). While I probably won't stop asking you about your thinking and encouraging you to do number talks at our dining room table, with this book finished, I am excited about more hours to hike, bike, picnic, and read with you. And to my husband, Andrew—thank you for believing that I could finish this beast! You never doubted me for a second. I appreciate more than you'll ever know the times you took the kids out to play to give me just a few more hours to write. I knew I married a man who would easily assume an equal share of household and childcare duties. But, in reality, you have taken on the lion's share of these while I pursued this book and my studies. I never could have finished *Math Workshop* without you. Thank you.

How to Use This Resource

▶ VIDEO CLIP Introduction

This introductory video clip gives glimpses of math workshop happening in grades K–5. As you watch the clip, consider these questions:

- What do you see happening that indicates math workshop is part of these classes?
- What is familiar to you?

- What surprises you?
- What do you have questions about?

To view this video clip, scan the QR code or access via mathsolutions.com/mathworkshopintro

What Is Math Workshop?

Math workshop is a model of instruction that allows all students to be engaged in the mathematics classroom—and for all students to realize their abilities as mathematicians. Math workshop is more of a philosophy than a lesson plan template. However, included in this resource are lesson plan examples and templates that will help you visualize what this will look like in your own classroom. Math workshop includes accessible mathematical tasks, open-ended problem solving, small-group instruction, student choice, and time for practice of important concepts throughout the year. All of this occurs in a way that makes mathematics enjoyable and meaningful for students and teachers.

> For more on the what and why of math workshop, see Chapter 1.

Why Math Workshop?

During math workshop, supporting all levels of student thinking is purposeful and plentiful—and is at the center of the entire philosophy of math workshop. In math workshop, differentiation doesn't just happen for students who are considered mathematically gifted or for students with special needs. Differentiation is for everyone, and this differentiated instruction is what allows our core instruction to be successful. Still not convinced? Math workshop is fun! Students like it. Teachers like it. It is a better way to spend time learning about mathematics content. As you read through this resource, you will see many ways in which math workshop will increase engagement and decrease anxiety. It saves time for teachers, provides teachers with more understanding of what their students understand, and makes learning math enjoyable and accessible.

Why *This* Resource?

When looking for resources to support reading and writing workshop, the options are countless. However, there seem to be fewer options for math workshop. Even as I scan my shelf of "go-to" resources, I find that many of my favorite titles focus on a component of learning stations or guided math groups. Each of these components has an important role in math workshop; however, I have found that it is a challenge implementing them without knowing the "whole picture" of a math workshop first. This resource does just that—providing five accessible steps to successfully implement all of (not just a part of) math workshop. It is intended to support you in your teaching and your thinking, ensuring that you are not alone in trying to determine how to make your math class the best it can be.

How This Resource Is Organized

Step 1: Understand Math Workshop

Chapter 1 is the first exciting step. This chapter gives you a quick overview of the *what*, *why*, and *when* of math workshop. Adult learners often need to understand why changes are happening. If that describes you, then this is a chapter that you will not want to miss. If you work in a school where you have to convince your administrator, your teammates, or parents why your mathematics instruction is looking different, then pull from this chapter to help make your case. This chapter provides the big picture—the one that you and your teammates will want to read in order to have a common understanding.

Step 2: Prepare Your Students for Math Workshop

Chapter 2 offers ideas and suggestions for how to set up your classroom—and your classroom culture—to begin math workshop. It is highly recommended that you read this chapter prior to implementing math workshop. It includes a section titled "Twenty Days to a Classroom Culture That Works," which introduces minilessons that support the communication and practice of expectations surrounding the workshop model. Facilitating these lessons and revisiting them when needed ensures that your students are well prepared for math workshop.

Step 3: Decide Your Math Workshop Structure

As stated previously, math workshop is a philosophy rather than a lesson plan template. The flexibility within the workshop model supports differentiation and allows you to make educated instructional decisions about what your students need most. **Chapters 3, 4, and 5** describe and compare the three different structures of math workshop: Task and Share (Chapter 3); Focus Lesson, Guided Math, and Learning Stations (Chapter 4); Guided Math and Learning Stations (Chapter 5). These chapters offer ideas to help you organize your math class in a meaningful and engaging way while making the most of the time that you have.

Reflect on It!

As you delve into this resource, look for how the philosophy of math workshop connects to your own philosophy for teaching mathematics. How is your current structure similar to math workshop? How is it different? You no doubt already have good things going on in your classroom. Make those connections! By implementing math workshop you are not changing your entire system for teaching mathematics. Rather, you are making modifications to improve your students' learning experience. At the end of most chapters, there are reflective questions. Use these questions to help make connections to your current work, reflect on what changes you may want to consider, and/or prompt meaningful discussions in study groups.

Step 4: Facilitate Your Math Workshop

Math workshop, regardless of the structure you are using, is made up of several components. **Chapter 6** offers various number sense routines to help you start each math class in an engaging and accessible way. These routines are

But It's Just Me . . .

You can do this solo. Math workshop is doable even if you don't have a team of teachers with whom to work. However, like any teaching practice, the opportunity to collaborate makes it even better.

often students' first impression of math class, and this chapter will help you to make that first impression a positive one.

Chapter 7 addresses engaging and meaningful learning stations. It discusses the importance of quality stations and choice, as well as ways to manage your classroom so that learning stations do not wreak havoc and disrupt instructional time.

Chapter 8 goes into detail about guided math groups. Often, the term *guided math* is used to describe an entire structure. This resource introduces guided math as one of the several important components of math workshop.

Student reflection is an important component of math workshop, and it is a component that easily gets overlooked in many math classes due to time. **Chapter 9** offers ideas for reflection opportunities that can transpire in a short amount of time and simultaneously provide the teacher with much needed information.

Chapter 10 brings the components and structures of math workshop together to show ways to make successful instructional decisions. A *Getting Started Checklist* ensures that you have considered the necessary actions to take in order to begin math workshop in your classroom. You will also find a sample lesson for how to first start so that you can "Go Slow to Go Fast!"

Step 5: Reflect On and Refine Your Math Workshop

In this section you'll find additional support critical to your use of math workshop. I like to think of these chapters as your own personal "instructional coach." When in doubt, turn to these chapters to think about things differently or find answers to your questions. You'll likely return to these chapters time and time again as you progress in making math workshop your own. **Chapter 11** has reflective questions to consider whether you are implementing math workshop solo, with a team, or as a whole school. You will also find suggested action steps to choose from, especially when you are feeling stuck or unsure of where to go next. **Chapter 12** is in the form of Frequently Asked Questions (FAQs). These were collected from my own experiences and the experiences of other teachers who have made a commitment to teach using math workshop.

Reproducibles

Downloadable reproducible templates are included for your use as you implement math workshop with students. These tools are provided to save you time. Use them in their original format or tweak them to make them your own. Download them at: www.mathsolutions.com/mathworkshopreproducibles.

How This Resource Is Meant to Be Read

This resource can be read from cover to cover. However, if you are reading this, then you are probably a teacher, instructional coach, or principal. You likely do not have the time to read this or anything else—especially if you are in the middle of a school year. This is one of the reasons that this resource breaks the information down into accessible, manageable steps. I get it! I know firsthand how busy you are. Rest assured, this resource will be well worth your time and will support you with the planning and the teaching of mathematics.

If you make the time to read this and implement the structures of math workshop, then you will gain time later. Math workshop is not only best for students; it is best for teachers, saving you time in the future. Math workshop makes teaching, planning, and learning easier in the end. It really does! As you read this and begin to make changes to your mathematics instruction, you may find it challenging at first. However, it will not take long for you to fall madly in love with math workshop. Your passion for mathematics will in turn be contagious in your classroom, and you will see a difference in your students' passion for learning mathematics. Math workshop is a game changer—for teachers and for students.

There Is No Time Like the Present!

I've read countless books on teaching over the years. I am always inspired as I read them and excited about the new possibilities for my classroom and for my school. When I finish a book, I put it in a "special" pile (on average about eight books high) categorized as "ideas to consider for next year." I've learned, however, that "next year" never really comes. Well, it does—but in the chaos that is a part of every start to a new year, that pile of ideas is forgotten. Is this something you can relate to?

I'm going to think optimistically and believe that you are already convinced that math workshop is going to be your new vehicle for math instruction in your classroom. Or, at the bare minimum, you think it is at least worth a try. If this is the case, I simply ask that you don't wait until next year to get started. Start today. Start now. Give it a shot. You won't regret it!

Streaming Video Clips

One of the best parts about this resource is that it includes authentic video clips of teachers and students in action. Seeing clips of actual teachers and students engaged in math workshop is the next best thing to observing the model in a classroom. These video clips help bring the words within the corresponding chapters to life. Note that the filming of these clips transpired in October. This should be encouraging; you too can have math workshop up and running within just one month of school! In addition, the teachers in these clips have between one and four years of experience with using math workshop in their classrooms. So you can rest easy knowing that while your first few math workshop lessons may look pretty messy, it won't take long for you to look and feel like an expert!

How to Access Online Video Clips

Readers have several options for accessing the video clips. Either scan the QR code (with a QR code reader app of your choice) that appears within the video clip section in the text or enter the corresponding URLs in your browser. If you would like to access all the clips at once, follow these instructions:

1. Go to mathsolutions.com/myvideos and click or tap the Create New Account button at the bottom of the Log In form.

2. Create an account, even if you have created one with the Math Solutions bookstore. You will receive a confirmation email when your account has been created.

3. Once your account has been created, you will be taken to the Product Registration page. Click Register on the product you would like to access (in this case, *Math Workshop*).

Key code: MWP

4. Enter key code **MWP** and click or tap the Submit Key Code button.

5. Click or tap the Complete Registration button.

6. To access videos at any time, visit your account page.

Quick Start!

Limited on time such that even getting through this "How to Use This Resource" section is challenging? I hear you and your need for a quick start. In a nutshell:

- Even if it is well into the school year and students are all getting along great as respectful community members, it is important to develop a sense of *mathematics community*. Do not pass over introducing the minilessons found in **Chapter 2**; they are critical to introducing the expectations of math workshop and developing your classroom culture.

- Select one of the three structures of math workshop (see **Chapters 3–5**) that is most similar to how you already teach. By choosing a structure that is similar to your own, you will more easily find connections.

- Let the magic begin! Observe, observe, observe. Then, reflect, reflect, reflect! Following the lesson, determine what went well and where students struggled. Use the reflection questions found in **Chapter 11** or consider the questions at the end of each chapter.

But . . . Go Slow to Go Fast!

Throughout my years of teaching and coaching, the message *Go Slow to Go Fast!* has become my mantra—and I think it's an important reminder after having just read the section titled "Quick Start."

As excited as you may be about getting started in using math workshop, I caution you to take it slowly. Start today, but don't change everything all at once. If you do and something fails, you won't know what piece of the change is causing the struggle. In the beginning of the school year we spend so much time on establishing systems and routines for turning in work, going to the restroom, walking to the cafeteria, reacting to a fire drill, and more. Being proactive and spending time on these routines makes the rest of the year go more smoothly. Establishing your system for learning mathematics should be no different. In order to successfully implement math workshop, make sure you've created a strong system of routines and procedures as well as developed a classroom community (see Chapter 2).

> Start today, but don't change everything all at once. If you do and something fails, you won't know what piece of the change is causing the struggle.

Video Clips by Chapter

CHAPTER	VIDEO CLIP	LENGTH	TEACHER AND GRADE	DESCRIPTION
2	2.1 Talking About Your Thinking	2:35	No Teacher Grade 5	In this clip, a team of fifth graders is engaged in a learning station activity, Toss 'n Talk, as part of math workshop. Students roll a sum, then they have to find the fraction equation that matches it.
2	2.2 Sharing Strategies	2:49	Ms. Wallace Grade 1	In this clip, Ms. Hrabak, as part of math workshop with fourth graders, facilitates a discussion on strategies used to solve the problem, *Jamie's family visited their grandmother, who lives 634 miles from their house. On the first day, they drove 319 miles. How many miles did they have left to drive the second day?*
2	2.3 Working Cooperatively	6:16	Ms. Lempp Grade 1	In this clip, Ms. Lempp facilitates a discussion with first graders on "working cooperatively" as part of preparing them for math workshop.
2	2.4 Using Manipulatives	4:33	Ms. Lempp Kindergarten	In this clip, Ms. Lempp gives kindergartners an opportunity to explore manipulatives they might use in math workshop.
2	2.5 Understanding the Guidelines for Math Workshop	6:06	Ms. Lempp Grade 2	In this clip, Ms. Lempp revisits, with a class of second graders, some of the expectations for math workshop.
3	3.1 The Task and Share Structure in Action	16:57	Ms. McGonigal Grade 3	This clip highlights excerpts from Ms. McGonigal's third-grade class as she facilitates a Task and Share math workshop structure.
4	4.1 The Focus Lesson, Guided Math, and Learning Stations Structure in Action	21:55	Ms. Hrabak Grade 4	This clip highlights excerpts from Ms. Hrabak's fourth-grade class as she facilitates a Focus Lesson, Guided Math, and Learning Stations math workshop structure.
5	5.1 The Guided Math and Learning Stations Structure in Action	18:34	Ms. Wallace Grade 1	This clip highlights excerpts from Ms. Wallace's first-grade class as she facilitates a Guided Math and Learning Stations math workshop structure.

CHAPTER	VIDEO CLIP	LENGTH	TEACHER AND GRADE	DESCRIPTION
6	6.1 Number Sense Routine: Number Talk Using Quick Images	5:12	Ms. Wallace Grade 1	In this clip, Ms. Wallace, to start math workshop with her first graders, chooses to do a number sense routine in the form of a number talk using quick images. To see how the rest of Ms. Wallace's math workshop unfolds after this routine, refer to Video Clip 5.1.
6	6.2 Number Sense Routine: Count Around	5:57	Ms. Griswold Kindergarten Ms. Hrabak Grade 4	In this clip, we see a number sense routine—count around—happening in two classrooms that are using it to begin math workshop: first in Ms. Griswold's kindergarten class and then in Ms. Hrabak's fourth-grade class. To see how the rest of Ms. Hrabak's math workshop unfolds after this routine, refer to Video Clip 4.1.
6	6.3 Number Sense Routine: Finger Patterns	5:29	Ms. Wallace Grade 1	In this clip, Ms. Wallace, to start math workshop with her first graders, facilitates a number sense routine, finger patterns.
7	7.1 The Power of Learning Stations	1:30	Ms. Lempp Mixed Grades	In this clip, the author Ms. Lempp talks about what makes a good learning station.
7	7.2 Introducing an Activity for a Learning Station	1:02	Ms. Robinson Grade 2	In this clip, Ms. Robinson briefly describes how she introduces an activity for a learning station to her second graders.
7	7.3 Ms. Wallace's Learning Stations	2:51	Ms. Wallace Grade 1	In this clip, Ms. Wallace shares with her first graders the learning stations for the day's math workshop.
7	7.4 Transitioning to Learning Stations	1:29	Ms. Robinson Grade 2	In this clip, Ms. Robinson transitions her class of second graders to the learning stations component of math workshop.
7	7.5 Math Menu: Dining Out	3:57	Ms. Callaway Grade 5	In this clip, Ms. Callaway transitions her fifth graders to their learning stations using a Dining Out math menu. We then see partners working together and reflecting on their learning stations.

(continued)

CHAPTER	VIDEO CLIP	LENGTH	TEACHER AND GRADE	DESCRIPTION
7	7.6 Math Menu: Must Do/Can Do	3:20	Ms. Hrabak Grade 4	In this clip, Ms. Hrabak facilitates a math workshop using a Must Do/Can Do menu. She also shares insights on what she does to ensure a successful math workshop. To see the rest of Ms. Hrabak's math workshop, refer to Video Clip 4.1.
7	7.7 Math Menu: Pocket Chart	2:46	Ms. Griswold Kindergarten	In this clip, Ms. Griswold uses a pocket chart during math workshop with her kindergarteners.
8	8.1 A Guided Math Group: What Is Symmetry?	3:12	Ms. Robinson Grade 2	In this clip, Ms. Robinson guides a small group of second graders through an activity focused on symmetry.
8	8.2 A Guided Math Group: Problem Solving	5:32	Ms. McGonigal Grade 3	In this clip, Ms. McGonigal guides a small group of third graders through a problem-solving task.
9	9.1 Student Reflection: Math Share	5:28	Ms. Griswold Kindergarten	In this clip, Ms. Griswold brings kindergartners together for a math share as the student reflection part of math workshop.
9	9.2 Student Reflection: Turn and Talk	4:10	Ms. Callaway Grade 5	In this clip, Ms. Callaway chooses to have fifth graders turn and talk as part of reflection time during math workshop.
10	10.1 Go Slow to Go Fast!	1:01	Ms. Lempp Mixed Grades	In this clip, the author Ms. Lempp advises teachers starting math workshop to "go slow to go fast."
12	12.1 Overcoming Roadblocks	1:15	Ms. Lempp Mixed Grades	Trying something new doesn't come without roadblocks. In this clip, the author Ms. Lempp shares two such roadblocks that teachers might encounter in math workshop and advises how to deal with them.

Video Clips by Grade, Including Demographics

Demographics   Rolling Valley Elementary School is home to about 575 students each school year. The school is located in a suburban neighborhood near Washington, DC, and is one of approximately 140 elementary schools in the district. Students at Rolling Valley thrive in the culturally diverse population with general education, special education, and English Language Learners (ELL) programs. Instruction is provided through a continuum of services integrated appropriately for the individual needs of each student.

GRADE	TEACHER	VIDEO CLIPS
K	**Ms. Griswold's** kindergarten class is made up of twenty-two eager mathematicians. Some of the students have a deep understanding of number sense, whereas others are still learning one-to-one correspondence to 10. Per Ms. Griswold's words, "My students hear many different languages outside of school, but in my class they are all learning to love the language of mathematics. Exploring the different areas of math workshop breaks down any language or learning barrier that we might come across in our diverse class. Math workshop allows each student to learn at his or her own pace and learn from each other."	2.4* 6.2 7.7 9.1

*These clips feature the author, **Ms. Lempp**.

(continued)

GRADE	TEACHER	VIDEO CLIPS
1	**Ms. Wallace's** first-grade class is a diverse group of twenty-four students ranging in learning styles and background knowledge. Ms. Wallace is in her fourth year of teaching; this is her second year fully implementing math workshop. Ms. Wallace states that her mathematics instruction has certainly changed because of math workshop; per her words, "It's not just me teaching directly to the kids and expecting a particular response. It's more of me giving students the choice in how they're learning and encouraging the dialogue among their peers."	2.2 5.1 6.1 6.3 7.3
2	**Ms. Robinson's** second-grade class is a wonderful mix of twenty-one different ways of thinking. Ms. Robinson's use of math workshop helps her identify and address the needs of her special education students, while simultaneously reaching the young scholars in her class. Per Ms. Robinson's words, "Every day in my classroom looks different, based upon students' needs within each unit."	2.5* 7.2 7.4 8.1

*These clips feature the author, **Ms. Lempp**.

GRADE	TEACHER	VIDEO CLIPS
3	**Ms. McGonigal's** third-grade class is a diverse group of twenty-three students representing seven different countries. Ms. McGonigal has been using and learning from math workshop for four years. After being introduced to math workshop, she completely changed her approach to math instruction. Her math block is now a time when students discover the big math ideas for themselves as she facilitates. Per Ms. McGonigal's words, "My math block not only became less exhausting for me to prepare, but much more meaningful for my students."	3.1 8.2
4	**Ms. Hrabak's** fourth-grade class is a diverse group of twenty-two students who enjoy solving math problems with their own strategies and sharing their thinking with classmates. More than seven different languages are spoken as the primary language at home. These students, although English is not their first language, are thriving in a math workshop environment. In fact, during math workshop, students are more comfortable talking because of the structures that are put in place to support their different learning styles. Per Ms. Hrabak's words, "I like seeing students come up with answers and think through the problems in a safe environment that fosters creative thinking and more choice."	2.3* 4.1 6.2 7.6

*These clips feature the author, **Ms. Lempp**.

(continued)

GRADE	TEACHER	VIDEO CLIPS
Grade 5	**Ms. Callaway's** fifth-grade class is a culturally diverse group of twenty-one students. Ms. Callaway has been teaching fifth grade for ten years. Per Ms. Callaway's words, "It didn't take long for me to see that using the math workshop approach made math more engaging and meaningful for all my fifth graders, regardless of their strengths and areas for improvement. With math workshop, I easily differentiate instruction to reach students' needs seamlessly and effectively."	2.1 7.5 9.2
Mixed Grades	These clips feature a mix of footage from two or more of the above grades.	7.1* 10.1* 12.1*

*These clips feature the author, **Ms. Lempp**.

Understand Math Workshop

This section answers the what, why, and when of math workshop. It explores what math workshop is (and is not!) and the key benefits of math workshop. It also answers a few important questions:

- What does math workshop look like?
- Why should I implement math workshop in my classroom?
- What are the benefits of using the math workshop model?
- What are the students doing?
- What is the teacher doing?

If you work in a school where you have to convince your administrator, your teammates, or parents why your mathematics instruction is looking different, then pull from this section to help make your case. This section provides the big picture—the one that you and your teammates will want to read in order to have a common understanding.

. . . .

Chapters in Step 1

Math Workshop: What, Why, and When?

Chapter 1

What Is Math Workshop?

In education, things seem to constantly be changing. As teachers, we wonder how long the latest new thing is going to be around. We wonder what will replace it. We wonder why the change has to happen and how much we will be asked to do. We often ask ourselves, *Do I really need to do this or will it be gone by next year? I'll outlast this latest new educational fad, right?*

> Though there is a definite philosophy to workshop teaching, it is not a curriculum. It is a structure amenable to any number of curricula and all topics (it is not hard to imagine a physical education workshop in the same model). It can—and should—look different in the hands of different teachers working in different schools. What is crucial is the focus on instruction, practice, and reflection, with the central idea that students learn best when they are doers, too.
>
> —Maggie Siena,
> *From Reading to Math*

It is fair to ask these same questions about math workshop. However, even if the term *math workshop* is replaced by a new fancy term one day, the philosophy of math workshop is here to stay. It is here to stay because math workshop, in its simplest definition, is *good mathematics instruction.*

What is good mathematics instruction? If we expect that our instruction is going to be strong, then we need to ensure that our instruction reaches all levels of learners; that students are engaged in daily, rich mathematical discussions; and that we allow ample time for students to grapple with mathematical ideas.

As stated in the How to Use This Resource section, math workshop is a model of instruction that allows for all students to be engaged in mathematics. It is more of a philosophy than a curriculum or lesson plan template. It includes accessible mathematical tasks, open-ended problem solving, small-group instruction, student choice, and time for practice of important concepts throughout the year.

Seven Math Workshop Characteristics

To answer the question "What is math workshop?" I find it easiest to first think about what math workshop *is not* as opposed to what it *is*. To do this, consider the seven characteristics of successful math workshops. (See Figure 1–1.) This list is not all-inclusive, and you may find that you want to add more characteristics as you finesse your own math workshop.

Let's explore each of these characteristics, and include a discussion of the research, in the hope of further clarifying our thinking around the definition of math workshop.

	MATH WORKSHOP *IS NOT* . . .	MATH WORKSHOP *IS* . . .
Characteristic 1	teachers doing most of the math.	students doing most of the math.
Characteristic 2	teachers assigning worksheets.	students making choices.
Characteristic 3	students quietly listening to only the teacher.	students enthusiastically talking about their mathematical thinking and reasoning with each other.
Characteristic 4	teachers showing and telling students how to solve problems.	teachers facilitating, clarifying, connecting, monitoring, and collecting data as students solve problems.
Characteristic 5	students working in isolation (sharing answers or strategies is cheating!).	students working collaboratively
Characteristic 6	teachers rescuing students when they struggle with challenging mathematics.	teachers allowing students to struggle with challenging mathematics.
Characteristic 7	teachers solely presenting to the whole class.	teachers working with small groups and/or individual students.

Figure 1–1. Seven characteristics of math workshop

▶ VIDEO CLIP Introduction, Revisited

Rewatch this clip, keeping in mind the seven math workshop characteristics (see Figure 1–1).

- Which characteristics of math workshop do you identify happening and/or being talked about in the clip?
- Which characteristics do you find most challenging to implement in your classroom?
- Is there a characteristic you would add to the list? If so, how would you describe it using the is not/is framework in Figure 1–1?

To view this video clip, scan the QR code or access via mathsolutions.com/mathworkshopintro

Characteristic 1: Math Workshop Is Students Doing Most of the Math

In a traditional model of mathematics instruction, the teacher does most of the talking—and subsequently the math. We want students to be doing the thinking and the learning, and to do so we need to engage them in doing the math.

Successful math workshops deeply engage students in the mathematics. This engagement might transpire through a number of structures; for example, some students may be working with the teacher in a small group while other students are exploring mathematics at learning stations. Whatever the arrangement is, it is not the teacher in front of the classroom doing the math; it is the students doing the math.

Characteristic 2: Math Workshop Is Students Making Choices

In math workshop you will not see teachers assigning (and students individually completing) worksheets. Rather, you will see students making choices. There is a wide range of choices students might be faced with; they may be choosing which learning station to explore, and/or they may have to decide what task to complete and who to work within each station. Students may choose what strategy to use to solve a problem and/or what manipulatives they use to support their thinking.

Patall, Cooper, and Robinson (2008) did a meta-analysis of forty-one studies in which they found a strong link between giving students choices and their intrinsic motivation for doing a task, their overall performance on the task, and their willingness to accept challenging tasks. Students who are given the choice of the activities, the choice in how long they spend on an activity, and the choice of what strategy to use to problem-solve are more invested and have more buy-in to their learning. However, remember to "go slow to go fast"—the transition from fewer to more choices should be gradual, sometimes spanning several months.

Characteristic 3: Math Workshop Is Students Enthusiastically Talking About Their Mathematical Thinking and Reasoning with Each Other

A classroom of students participating in math workshop is rarely a quiet room. Student discourse is encouraged and respectful dialogue is expected. Students talk about their thinking, share with one another, listen to one another, and learn from each other. Students value the knowledge of their peers and look to one another as supportive colleagues in their learning environment.

Zwiers and Crawford (2011) list many advantages of conversations that transcend the mathematics classroom; a few are included here.

Conversation . . .

- builds academic language;
- builds vocabulary;
- builds oral language and communication skills;
- builds critical thinking skills;
- promotes different perspectives and empathy;
- fosters creativity;
- fosters skills for negotiating meaning and focusing on a topic;
- builds content understanding;
- cultivates connections;
- builds relationships;
- makes lessons more culturally relevant;
- fosters engagement and motivation;
- builds confidence and academic identity
- fosters choice, ownership, and control over thinking; and
- builds student voice and empowerment.

Wow! Isn't that list exactly what we dream about for all of our students? After looking at the list, I wonder why I would ever want to walk into a quiet classroom again.

Characteristic 4: Math Workshop Is Teachers Facilitating, Clarifying, Connecting, Monitoring, and Collecting Data as Students Solve Problems

As teachers our roles may differ based on which math workshop structure we are using (see Chapters 3–5). However, regardless of the structure we choose to use, there are four roles teachers take on in math workshop:

1. the teacher as facilitator,
2. the teacher as clarifier and connector,
3. the teacher as monitor, and
4. the teacher as data collector.

Let's take a moment to look at each of these roles a bit more in depth.

Role 1: The teacher as facilitator At a certain point in my teaching career, after attending several conferences and participating in professional learning opportunities, I committed to telling less and asking more. To do this, I started asking questions and probing for students' understanding. The effect it had on my students was remarkable. At first, students responded with frustration, exclaiming, "Just tell me what you want me to do!" However, it wasn't long before students felt motivated by the opportunity to be problem solvers and excited by the chance to explore problems. I started to see students picking up on my questions and using them with each other!

A teacher once told me that in the beginning of her use of math workshop, when she would ask the question, "How do you know?" her students would immediately change their answer because they assumed that they must be wrong. But by asking this question frequently and consistently with every student, her students started to ask *her*, "Don't you want to know how I know?"

Some questions to consider asking students to probe their thinking or help them get unstuck might include:

- What information do you know?
- What have you done so far?
- Would your strategy work with a different set of numbers?
- How might you prove this to your peers?
- Can you make a model to prove this?
- What other methods might have worked?
- Have you considered all the possibilities? How do you know?

> As teachers, when we act as facilitators, we encourage independence, responsibility, and risk taking in students.

As teachers, when we act as facilitators, we encourage independence, responsibility, and risk taking in students. Students come to realize that the teacher believes in them and their ability to solve problems. The onus is on the students to participate in the learning experience, and with that, students have a more solid understanding of the content and are not simply regurgitating the teacher's steps.

Role 2: The teacher as clarifier and connector A second role of the teacher during math workshop is to clarify students' ideas and find connections. Our students are still kids; they might not always be able to explain what they are thinking or find the words to express their strategy. During these times, our role as clarifier and connector is critical. We can ask thoughtful questions, encourage students to talk to one another, ask if students agree or disagree (the use of talk moves is helpful), and provide the appropriate vocabulary when paraphrasing a student's thinking. To encourage connections, we can use meaningful, real-world examples, another mathematics concept, or another content area. Finding those connections and helping students to see them creates important learning moments—and instills curiosity. Just think, how can students be curious if they are focused only on memorizing facts and procedures?

Do not make the mistake, however, of confusing your role as clarifier and connector with taking over a student's thinking. Even the most well-intentioned teachers can fall into doing this, especially due to time pressures. We see the time ticking away and we jump in, take the pencil out of the student's hand, move the manipulatives around for the student, and essentially show the student how to do it. We must be aware of and refrain from this behavior.

> "Finding connections and helping students to see them creates important learning moments—and instills curiosity. Just think, how can students be curious if they are focused only on memorizing facts and procedures?"

Role 3: The teacher as monitor During math workshop, as teachers we should monitor students' participation, being on the lookout for students who might not be engaged, who might be "hiding" from doing the task at their learning station, or who might be displaying passive behavior. We should note which students' voices we hear the most and encourage all students' voices to be heard. To encourage more student participation, have students turn to partners more frequently; getting students to interact with a partner first will help them feel more comfortable when it comes to talking with more classmates.

Role 4: The teacher as data collector As teachers we know our students' strengths, weaknesses, and learning styles; to get this information we use multiple forms of assessment, and collect some form of data each and every day. During math workshop, we might consider taking anecdotal notes. Anecdotal notes

- are recorded during math class, especially during guided group time;
- help us make instructional decisions for the entire class and for individual students;
- support us when we need to assign grades and conference with parents;
- help us create small groups for future math workshops; and
- remind us of the great things that are going on in the minds of our students long after the day's workshop takes place.

If you are comfortable taking notes about student performance during reading workshop, then this role will likely seem more natural to you as part of math workshop. However, you may wonder what to write down. See Chapter 8 for examples of anecdotal records.

Characteristic 5: Math Workshop Is Students Working Collaboratively

The important work of mathematics is not done in isolation. In a math workshop you will see students collaborating to solve problems and make sense of the mathematics. In the primary grades, students often feel more comfortable collaborating in pairs, whereas in upper elementary grades, larger groups of four or five students may be preferred.

Collaboration is a twenty-first-century skill that is not fostered enough in mathematics classrooms. Students are often put in pairs or small groups to work together in other content areas; however, mathematics, for most, is still a very isolated subject that is presented as black or white, right or wrong. When students talk to one another, they improve their own reasoning and are exposed to other strategies. When students work together, their learning increases. And they don't just learn mathematics—they learn how to work in groups, monitor their own behavior, and interact with peers who have different experiences or ideas.

> When students work together, their learning increases. And they don't just learn mathematics—they learn how to work in groups, monitor their own behavior, and interact with peers who have different experiences or ideas.

Characteristic 6: Math Workshop Is Teachers Allowing Students to Struggle with Challenging Mathematics

We have all seen it—students who shoot their hand up for help just seconds after you've given an assignment. All I can think in that moment is that they could not possibly have a question so soon. After all, they did not even have a chance to get started. When I approach such students, they usually say the words that I dread the most in a classroom: "I don't get it!" At this moment, it can be easy for a teacher to tell (or show) the first step, just to get students started. However, in doing this, we are stealing from students the opportunity to struggle. And we are sending a harsh message: *You can't do this without me.* There are also the students who do the opposite: those who quietly sit back and wait for someone else to solve the problem. These students know that someone else will do the "heavy lifting" for them if they just wait long enough.

In math workshop students develop the mindset that they are capable of doing great things in mathematics. As teachers, we support them in persevering through challenging problems; we recognize that a student's struggle is a part of the learning process. We want students to realize that a part of the process is getting wrong answers and learning from those experiences. After all, if it were all easy, would there really be any learning going on?

Seeley (2009) advocates for *constructive struggling*, a term that refers to the positive place students reach when presented with engaging and challenging problems. "As students engage in the constructive struggling needed for some of these problems, they learn that perseverance, in-depth analysis, and critical thinking are valued in mathematics (90).

In order for students to truly understand math, they need to explore it for themselves and have ownership of the strategies that they use. As teachers, we often tell students to "show your work." Yet, what we are really asking them to do is to "show *my* work"—meaning show me the way that I showed you how to solve it. In that situation, math simply becomes a procedure in the student's mind. And, if math is equal to a procedure, then students think that memorizing procedures will equate to their success in mathematics. Just think about it . . . those for whom math is simply something to memorize start off by memorizing 100 addition facts and then the correlated subtraction facts. Such students then memorize a traditional algorithm for addition and subtraction with regrouping. Moving on to third grade, these same students memorize 144 multiplication facts and the correlated division facts, how to multiply by two-digit factors, and the process for long division. Whew! That is a lot, and we have not even made it to fifth grade. No wonder so many students feel that math is too difficult!

However, there is an alternative. Instead, allow the opportunity for student exploration of strategies (and this may very well include struggle!). The methods that they use could be shared with the class, discussed, put under scrutiny, and revised. Students defend their strategy, choose to abandon their strategy if it lacks consistent results, or find another, more useful strategy. True number sense will allow a student to have a variety of strategies to use at their disposal. The thing that makes students successful is that they have the knowledge of when to use the one that best fits their purpose.

Characteristic 7: Math Workshop Is Teachers Working with Small Groups and/or Individual Students
In math workshop, while students are working collaboratively in learning stations or delving into rich problem solving with one another, the teacher is working with small groups of students or individuals. These small groups, referred to in this book as guided math

> "In math workshop students develop a mindset that they are capable of doing great things in mathematics."

groups, are determined by what the teacher has observed as well as other data points. The teacher may also meet with one student during this time (considered a math conference) as a way to help clarify thinking or interject about a misconception.

Math workshop teachers recognize that there are a lot of students in the classroom, and no two students are exactly alike. Presenting to the whole class at once is like shooting for the middle. However, in shooting for the middle, you are missing many other students—those who may be struggling or have gaps and those who may be in need of enrichment. Of course, as teachers we try to do in-the-moment adaptations of our lessons based on the questions students ask or the facial expressions they make. Still, we are left trying to adapt for many students. By getting these students into smaller groups, we are able to find out more about what each student knows and does not yet know. As teachers we are able to make those adjustments more quickly, and we are better able to address the individual needs of students. In this way, differentiation can take place.

Three Math Workshop Structures

You may already be feeling that the seven math workshop characteristics match your own philosophy about what math class should include. You might be recognizing how different this feels from your own experiences as a student in mathematics. You might also be wondering how these characteristics look when you are considering a unit or lesson. A successful math workshop continually integrates these seven characteristics into an effective structure. You might already have a structure or structures in use; this resource focuses on three math workshop structures that I've found most successful in my instruction and coaching. Figure 1–2 provides an overview of these three structures. These three structures are discussed in greater detail in the section "Step 3: Decide Your Math Workshop Structure." It's intended that you become well-versed in all three structures and comfortable moving from one to the other, selecting which structure best matches your students' needs at any given time.

MATH WORKSHOP: TASK AND SHARE		MATH WORKSHOP: FOCUS LESSON, GUIDED MATH, AND LEARNING STATIONS		MATH WORKSHOP: GUIDED MATH AND LEARNING STATIONS	
5–10 minutes	NUMBER SENSE ROUTINE	5–10 minutes	NUMBER SENSE ROUTINE	5–10 minutes	NUMBER SENSE ROUTINE
30 minutes	MATH TASK	15 minutes	FOCUS LESSON	45 minutes	GUIDED MATH / LEARNING STATIONS
		30 minutes	GUIDED MATH / LEARNING STATIONS		
20–25 minutes	TASK SHARE WITH STUDENT REFLECTION	5–10 minutes	STUDENT REFLECTION	5–10 minutes	STUDENT REFLECTION

Figure 1–2. Three math workshop structures: an overview

Reflect on It!

Do you already use reading or writing workshop in your classroom? How about guided reading groups? Writing conferences? If so, what connections are you making to math? What are students doing in your classroom while you work with small groups or individuals?

Why Math Workshop?

Why implement math workshop in your classroom? In a nutshell, math workshop

- provides students with differentiated instruction: instruction that is targeted and based on individual student understanding;
- encourages independence, responsibility, and risk taking in students and creates mathematicians who have a solid foundation of number sense, which leads to a conceptual understanding of mathematics; and
- provides students with engaging learning experiences that promote mathematical thinking, discourse, and a positive disposition toward mathematics.

Let's address these reasons for "Why math workshop?" further by exploring the benefits, specifically the benefits of:

1. differentiation,
2. small-group instruction,
3. student choice,
4. discourse, and
5. continued practice of the big ideas.

The Benefits of Differentiation

Differentiation is defined as classroom practice that has a balanced emphasis on individual students and course content. It should not be merely regarded as a buzzword in education; in math workshop, differentiation is purposeful and plentiful. Differentiation is at the center of the entire philosophy of math workshop. In math workshop, differentiation doesn't just happen for students who are considered mathematically gifted or for students with special needs; differentiation happens for everyone.

Tomlinson and Imbeau (2010) state that the modifications of four curriculum-related elements are at the core of differentiation—content, process, product, and affect. When considering differentiation of the *content*, as teachers we must consider district, state, and national standards; student understandings based on assessment data; and whether a student has an Individualized Education Plan (IEP). When differentiating *process*, we need to allow for multiple ways for students to make sense of the content. To differentiate the *product*, we need to give students a variety of ways to demonstrate their knowledge. When considering *affect*, we observe student behavior and work to drive students in a positive direction. The math workshop model of instruction takes all these modifications into account.

As math workshop teachers, we understand the mathematics, and we are thoughtful about how to support the learning of the *content*. We carefully examine assessment data, get to know students well, and make intentional adjustments in order to meet the needs of all students in the classroom. We are thoughtful about *process* and *product*; we create a classroom community that respects a variety of choices, perspectives, and strategies, and we encourage and celebrate diverse thinking. And we are attuned to *affect*; we hold a strong belief that we have the capability to make an impact on student learning and students have the capability to be successful in mathematics.

Compare this to a more traditional model of instruction: the teacher is standing in front of the classroom, showing students how to do the math. Every child is expected to work on the same practice problem, every child is assigned the same worksheet, and every child is given the same test. In this model of instruction, a small amount of differentiation may take place. The teacher may gauge the understanding of the class based on student responses and facial expressions. She may adjust the numbers that students are using, try to say it in another way, or modify students' questions. However, trying to do this in the moment with dozens of students can be a daunting—if not impossible—job.

What about the child who is good at hiding during math class? You know that child; you might have been him or her as a student yourself. That child does nothing outwardly disobedient to show that he is not listening or paying attention. That child may even make eye contact and smile. However, that child does not intend to answer any questions, and often feels lost during the whole-class lesson. That child chooses instead to wait it out. He waits the teacher out, and he waits out his friends. He knows that someone else will answer the question, and then he will be off the hook—he will be safe. Such a student might exhibit other avoidance behaviors like sharpening a pencil that is already sharp, throwing away a tissue that wasn't really even used, or using the restroom even though he doesn't have to go. As teachers we likely can all identify these "hiding child" behaviors during our math lessons.

In a traditional classroom, we are not necessarily seeing bad teachers. However, we are most likely seeing average teachers. In *Tools for Engagement: Managing Emotional States for Learner Success*, Eric Jensen (2003) describes the difference between an average teacher and a great one:

An average teacher may be reaching, at any given time, fifty to seventy percent of the audience. A great teacher may be reaching, at any given time, fifty to seventy percent of the audience, *but a different fifty to seventy percent each time!* In other words, the great teacher uses a variety of activities and instructional methods to ensure that they reach different learners at different times. Over the course of a week or a month, the great teacher will eventually reach all learners. The average teacher, however, will still be reaching the same learners over and over again. The average teacher, too, will lump learners by their ability into a bell curve at grading time, convinced that the differences among learners are because of differences in effort or ability, not because of teaching! (22)

Students come into class with a range of background knowledge, interests, strengths, socioeconomic circumstances, and languages—it's no wonder addressing the needs of all learners can often feel overwhelming. For many of us as teachers, differentiating in literacy is clear. We choose a different level text or a different genre in order to support student learning. In mathematics, however, we often struggle with the idea of differentiation. Math workshop is here to help. It provides the mathematics instruction that students need when they need it by creating small groups for learning, offering student choice, and allowing enough time for students to grapple with a concept by spiraling or looping back.

When differentiation is taking place, students are more actively engaged in the lesson. Students who are engaged in their learning will undoubtedly be more successful. When engagement goes up and anxiety goes down, learning happens!

Reflect on It!

How are you meeting individual student needs in math class? What are your successes and challenges with differentiation?

The Benefits of Small-Group Instruction

Small-group instruction is important for many reasons. Fountas and Pinnell (2001) explain in their book on guided reading that small-group instruction allows for appropriate instruction for a diverse class of learners, improves the confidence of students and increases expectations for academic success. The same can be said for math. By placing students into small groups, as teachers we can more easily gather an abundance of information on each student. This is overwhelmingly difficult when faced with trying to gather information at once with dozens of students. It is during small-group instruction that we get to know so much more about student thinking. We get to know students' readiness levels, approaches to tasks, learning preferences/styles, the vocabulary that they possess, and what they connect to in real life and previous mathematics. It is during this time that we can also evaluate student understanding, take anecdotal notes, and make mental notes about future grouping possibilities. It is easy for most of us as teachers to see that in small groups in reading, we are able to provide "just-right" text. How can we carry that same philosophy over to mathematics?

The math workshop model of instruction encourages small-group interactions. Small groups in turn provide students with the opportunity for "just-right" math instruction and the opportunity to problem solve with their peers. In two of the math workshop structures presented in this book, the Focus Lesson, Guided Math, and Learning Stations Structure (Chapter 4) and the Guided Math and Learning Stations Structure (Chapter 5), the teacher pulls *guided math groups* for small-group instruction. However small-group instruction does not only take place during guided math groups. That would be like saying that students can only learn from the teacher. And our philosophy in math workshop is that students will learn from one another when given the opportunity to share and discuss. Hence we must not forget that small-group instruction also takes place during *learning stations* and other group activities happening in math workshop.

There are also times when a teacher will find the smallest of group instruction, *conferencing*, beneficial. This component of math workshop entails just one student meeting individually with the teacher. There are times when you will want to touch base with one student to conduct an interview-style of assessment, clarify a student's thinking, or help to correct a misconception. This one-on-one meeting can be a powerful time to observe student understanding and assess students' needs. This is a personal time between teacher and student—a time when you can more deeply communicate your confidence in a student's ability. While meeting one-on-one with students may seem like a luxury in our busy schedules, sometimes this one-on-one interaction is crucial—and a math workshop model of instruction helps make it possible.

Think about the following scenario in kindergarten: I want to know if my students can count to one hundred. I can give them a pencil and a blank hundreds chart and have them fill it in. Or, I can conference with these students for just a couple of minutes to determine if they can count forward from zero to one hundred. What is more efficient? It is well worth my time to have a few minutes with each child, listen to each child count, listen to when and where they hesitate, and take notes about their progress. I can even use a simple check-off chart. (See Figure 1–3 on the next page.)

> Small groups provide students with the opportunity for "just-right" math instruction and the opportunity to problem solve with their peers.

	COUNTS FROM 0–10	COUNTS FROM 0–30	COUNTS FROM 0–75	COUNTS FROM 0–100
Sally	✓	✓		
Suri	✓	✓	✓	
Marcos	✓	✓	✓	✓
Stefan	✓			

Figure 1–3. Recording observations during one-on-one conferencing

Reflect on It!

In *Simplifying Response to Intervention*, Buffum, Mattos, and Weber (2010) explain that differentiating instruction and small-group instruction are the most important steps a school can make to improve core instruction. How can knowing this help your school make the change to math workshop?

> Math workshop offers a social environment in which small groups of students switch on their brains and work with one another and with the teacher. In this social environment, students are more engaged, make more connections, and are more open to learning.

Cathy Seeley in *Faster Isn't Smarter* (2015) explains that "student engagement involves switching on a student's brain so that she is interacting with mathematics in deep, thoughtful, and meaningful ways" (218). In small groups, whether in guided math with the teacher or in learning stations with their peers, students' time on task is maximized, as is the opportunity to talk to one another. Small groups promote social interaction—an important part of the learning process. Most of the learning that we have done in our lives has been done through social interactions with others. Why not make this the case in mathematics? Why is learning in mathematics often so isolating? Instead, math workshop offers a social environment in which small groups of students "switch on their brains" and work with one another and with the teacher. In this social environment, students are more engaged, make more connections, and are more open to learning.

The Benefits of Student Choice

Earlier in the chapter, we visited the idea of choice when it comes to understanding the "what" of math workshop. Dacey, Lynch, and Salemi (2013) explain that when students are able to make choices, having a sense of control in the classroom, it will lead to an increase in interest and a positive attitude in class. When students have choice, they feel more confident and more competent. As teachers, we send a message of respect to students when we provide them with options.

Many teachers steer away from student choice for fear of complete chaos in the room. Choice does not mean that students can do whatever they want, wherever they want, and with whomever they want. Think about this in the context of toddlers; we won't let them wear a swimsuit outside in the winter, but we can offer them a choice between the blue sweater or green sweater. This choice gives them a sense of respect and validates their feelings by allowing them to make the selection. The same is true for students in math workshop.

It's important to make expectations and procedures clear, practice the routines, and provide feedback to students in making appropriate choices. In turn, choices empower students, help them take ownership of their learning, and keep students engaged and excited about the mathematics they are exploring.

Choices You Can Offer Students

- Which topics to study
- Which tasks to complete
- What materials to use
- With whom to partner
- Where to work
- How long to work on a particular task
- The order in which to complete assignments
- How to represent and present ideas
- How to demonstrate what is understood (Dacey, Lynch, and Salemi, 2013)

The Benefits of Discourse

I've often heard it said that the person doing the most talking is the person doing the most learning. In reflecting on this during my early years of teaching I came to the rather disturbing realization that the person doing the most talking during math class was me. I was working very hard to show the mathematics another way, to say it another way in order to get each and every one of my students nodding their heads in understanding. And when they didn't all nod, I thought that if I did it just one more time, then maybe, just maybe, they would all understand it.

What I failed to recognize for some time was that as long as I was talking and doing the math, the students were neither talking about the math nor doing the math. And it needed to be the other way around—discourse—classroom discussion—is essential to learning. Chapin, O'Connor, and Anderson

(2009) state that "when a teacher succeeds in setting up a classroom in which students feel obligated to listen to one another, to make their own contributions clear and comprehensible, and to provide evidence for their claims, that teacher has set in place a powerful context for student learning" (9). I couldn't agree more!

A classroom community that supports diverse thinking, encourages cognitive conflict, and respects various strategies and solutions is a classroom full of learners. Getting students to explain their thinking helps them better understand the mathematics. Through discourse, students are exposed to alternate strategies and receive feedback on their reasoning. And—may it be of no surprise—all of this happens during math workshop.

One of our fears as teachers is that, when encouraging more discussion in our classrooms, the amount of talk will increase but it won't be about anything of educational significance. After all, we don't want students to talk if it means being off task. We want the discussion to move students forward in their mathematical thinking. We want discussion that promotes engagement, helps students reason, and supports students in making meaning of the mathematics.

Another fear we may have is that students, when engaging in talk, will share the wrong answer with each other. *What if they are talking, but they are telling each other the wrong thing?* A teacher once shared this concern with me, and we decided to think about what happens when the accurate "thing" is shared. Does this mean that all students then know how to do it? If only it were that easy, right? We concluded that it's okay if students, while grappling with important mathematical ideas, make errors and discuss these errors with one another.

To help alleviate fears when it comes to discourse—and simultaneously address the reality that many students struggle with *how* to talk about mathematics—consider using talk moves. These moves, as described in *Talk Moves* (Chapin, O'Connor, and Anderson 2013), transition students from simply talking to sharing, discussing, arguing, listening, reflecting, and self-monitoring.

While these talk moves are not the only "moves" that can be used to support classroom discourse, they serve as a good place to start. Begin by choosing one of the *talk moves* and using it more often in your classroom. This helps students start to value the thoughts of others, see one another and themselves as valuable contributors to the learning that is taking place, and successfully use talk in math workshop.

> To help alleviate fears when it comes to discourse—and simultaneously address the reality that many students struggle with *how* to talk about mathematics—consider using talk moves.

The Benefits of Continued Practice of the Big Ideas

I've sat with countless school teams while we plan for mathematics. As teachers we realize that we have a huge curriculum and a wide range of students, many of whom may not be prepared for the curriculum being introduced. One of the biggest concerns is moving on too quickly when we feel that students still need time to grapple with the mathematics on hand. However, the huge amount of curriculum presses the need to cover more in a short period of time. I've often heard teachers say, *If I don't move on, I will never be able to get it all in*. We all recognize that students need time to explore mathematics, and that not every child will master a concept at the same time. In math workshop, learning stations allow continuous exposure and practice of the big ideas in mathematics.

While working with a third-grade team that had not yet embraced math workshop, I learned that the teachers were concerned about moving on to measurement and data. After all, they still had so many students who needed more time to dig into multiplication. And they had several students who were struggling with understanding subtraction with regrouping. The teachers felt they had two choices: to remain on multiplication until everyone "had it," even if that meant skipping other portions of the curriculum; or to move on to measurement and hope that the students "got" multiplication when they moved to fourth grade. This group of dedicated, hardworking teachers was not happy with either of these options. Through the review of formative assessment data and careful planning, they decided instead to put students who still needed some support with multiplication and/or subtraction into small guided math groups focused on such. They also created learning stations around engaging activities that students could collaboratively work on to help with the concepts of multiplication and subtraction with regrouping. In the next three weeks, the teachers moved a great number of their students forward in their understanding. When we met again, the teachers decided which learning stations would remain a part of their classroom choices and regrouped the students based on new data.

Through math workshop, students have opportunities to continually practice what is being taught. Math workshop reinforces the fact that the development of mathematical ideas takes place throughout the year and is not isolated to one particular unit or lesson. Math workshop helps support students in making connections among mathematics concepts—remember

> I've often heard teachers say, *If I don't move on, I will never be able to get it all in*. We all recognize that students need time to explore mathematics, and that not every child will master a concept at the same time. In math workshop, learning stations allow continuous exposure and practice of the big ideas in mathematics.

that short-term performance of a mathematical idea should not be confused with conceptual understanding.

In turn, a math workshop teacher better knows which students are showing mastery of the content and which have yet to do so thanks to the time math workshop lends to observing and assessing student performance. Students who need more support in mastering a skill can be supported in guided math groups. In addition, the teacher can intentionally choose learning stations that offer students meaningful practice with those skills.

When Does Math Workshop Happen?

Math workshop happens each and every day in your classroom. Making math workshop work for you will be easier if your team works collaboratively and there is a well-established professional learning community at your school. DuFour and Eaker (1998) remind us that traditional teachers work in isolation while those teachers who are a part of a professional learning community share ideas about teaching practices. However, even if you are teaching solo in a one-room schoolhouse, implementing math workshop is still doable and worth it. Once you start on this path, it's likely you'll never go back.

> Math workshop happens each and every day in your classroom.

Remember, math workshop is more of a philosophy than a prescribed lesson plan. The beauty of math workshop is that it becomes a part of who you are as a mathematics teacher. When we use math workshop as our model of instruction, we believe in a student's right to a deep, conceptually based education. We believe that students learn from exploration. We believe that all students are bright, talented, and wonderful thinkers. We believe that students can and should learn from one another through collaboration and rich mathematical discourse. And we believe in the power of preparing students to become problem solvers!

Math Workshop: Voices from Experience

Finally, don't just take my word for it. In fact, don't just take the researchers' words for it, either. On the following pages you'll find the voices of teachers, parents, and, more importantly, students expressing the benefits of math workshop. They are hooked. With time, you will be too! You won't just be teaching mathematics in a math workshop model because of what is said in this book; you will be convinced that math workshop is a better way for all students to learn and a more effective and efficient way for all teachers to teach.

Voices from Experience: Teachers

"Math workshop allows students to engage in cooperative learning and create their own understanding of complex math concepts. Students are excited to be doing math and I always seem to hear a little cheer when I tell them to get ready for math workshop."

—first-grade teacher

"Math workshop has given new life to my math class. My kids are so much more engaged and excited about math now that we use math workshop. They also have more confidence because workshop encourages community, and that sense of community encourages active participation and willingness to share ideas."

—fourth-grade teacher

"I realize that before, I wasn't giving my students enough credit. They can do so much more than I thought they could. I never would have seen that if I hadn't used the math workshop model."

—fifth-grade teacher

Voices from Experience: Parents

"My child used to hate math. Now she loves it! It is the first homework that she wants to do when she gets home from school. She always has so much to say about the games that she played in math that day. I love that she isn't so insecure anymore."

—parent of a sixth grader

"I never liked math as a kid. So it didn't really faze me that my son didn't like math either. Then, this year, math was different. It seemed fun! He likes the class, and I've seen better grades in math than I have ever seen before."

—parent of a fifth grader

"My son probably has a better understanding of math than I do. He seems to under-stand why it all works. I was always good at math, but now I recognize that I really didn't understand why I was doing what I was doing. I just did it and I got the right answer. I never questioned why."

—parent of a third grader

Voices from Experience: Students

"I don't like math, but I love math workshop! It is way more fun! It is my favorite part of the day."

—first-grade student

"I was never good at math before, but now I am. I'm really good at math now."

—fourth-grade student

"Math like this is fun. I get to work with my friends, and sometimes they can explain it to me when I don't understand it. My teacher helps me so much, and I'm not afraid of doing it wrong anymore. I never liked math before, but this year it is one of my favorites. My favorite thing about math is when I get to work with the teacher in guided math. I always feel better after."

—fifth-grade student

"I like having a choice of how I do my math center."

—first-grade student

"Math makes my brain think a lot in a lot of different ways."

—first-grade student

"I can't believe we get to move around the room! We always used to sit at our desks during math time."

—fourth-grade student

"We get to choose different math activities! Usually we just do worksheets."

—fourth-grade student

"I love getting to solve problems with my friends and see how different our ways to get the answers are."

—fourth-grade student

Voices from Experience: My Story

There was a time not so long ago when I taught math to my students exactly the way it had been taught to me. I stood in front of the class, announced that we would be learning about _____. I showed them how to do it on the chalkboard/whiteboard/overhead/interactive whiteboard, and then I had them work on a few problems on their own. I threw in a cool math trick or two to make it "easier" for students. I had students use manipulatives to work it out. The quiz was on Friday, and our new material would start the following Monday.

At some point in my career I realized that this environment was not successfully supporting my students. Students were regurgitating my way of doing math rather than persevering through their own struggle of mathematics and developing their own conceptual understanding. As a result, my students were able to mimic the steps day after day, but their math understanding was not making it to long-term memory. Often students had forgotten what do to by the time the test came around. I had to make a change.

I learned early on that many educational gurus had already figured out the best environment for students to learn reading and writing. But it took me several years to borrow these ideas, mold them, and make the connection to how this system could work in my mathematics classroom.

Irene C. Fountas and Gay Su Pinnell are widely known to elementary school teachers for their knowledge and understanding of reading and writing workshop. So, for many years, I worked to establish learning stations and small-group instruction that reflected this workshop model. Since most of my teaching ideas have been "borrowed" from the countless amazing teachers who I have worked with over the years, I proudly say thank you to all those who have come before me for providing me with wonderful ideas that have made instruction engaging and purposeful for students.

In what ways do you make your math instruction engaging and purposeful for students?

I started off using math workshop in a fourth-grade classroom in North Carolina. I didn't call it a workshop then. I created fun and exciting math games for students to work on with partners or small groups, and I pulled groups of students or individuals to work on specific math skills. It wasn't perfect. Upon reflection, I didn't choose the most powerful math activities. I didn't take full advantage of pretest data to help me form small groups. I also didn't have a system for communicating options to students.

When I moved on to teaching in a middle school, I was confronted by something that I didn't have to use in elementary school—a textbook! It would have been easy for me to start on page 1 and move on, page by page, through the book. However, the vast differences in mathematics experiences of my students made it abundantly clear that I was not going to reach even half of them using the textbook as it was. So I decided to use the same system that I had used when I taught fourth graders. I created learning stations for students so that I could simultaneously work with small groups or individuals. I created small groups, this time being more intentional about whom I worked with and what we worked on.

Then an amazing thing happened. I started working at a school that was built around the idea of professional learning communities. Soon I was not alone in creating learning stations. I collaborated with a wonderful group of teachers who shared ideas, created common assessments, and worked to make every day in the classroom a positive experience for students. What I was doing all alone for years started to feel much more doable as we addressed each unit together as a team. It was with this group of teachers that I learned more about myself as an educator, further questioned my teaching techniques, and challenged myself to take more risks—stepping further away from the traditional model of mathematics instruction. We selected learning stations and wrote lessons, and then we reflected on what went well and what didn't.

> I worked with teachers to try out math workshop at every grade level. Math workshop was as equally successful in the kindergarten classroom as it was in the middle school classroom.

We let go of the stations that were not making the impact that we had hoped for. Each year, our collection of engaging and powerful stations grew. While planning never got easy (I don't know a teacher who can say that it is), it did get easier!

I continued doing this in my own classroom for the next few years, tweaking my lessons and stations, and reflecting on what was making the most difference in my students. I believed so much in this model of instruction that soon after taking a math coach job, I worked with teachers to try out math workshop at every grade level. Math workshop was as equally successful in the kindergarten classroom as it was in the middle school classroom. Were there some differences? Sure! However, some things were the same regardless of the age of the students. Students were enjoying mathematics (some for the first time ever), students were making greater strides in mathematics, and students were helping one another in their transformation to mathematicians.

As a math coach, I've had the pleasure of working with thousands of teachers to either implement or improve their use of math workshop in several schools and school systems across the country. I've seen an increase in teacher efficacy, and I've seen smiling faces of the students who are instructed with a math workshop approach.

Connecting the Chapter to Your Practice

- From what you know about math workshop at this point, how is your classroom similar to math workshop? How might it be different?

- What pieces of math workshop already fit with your philosophy or current structure?

- What is something that you want to change about your current structure of mathematics instruction?

Prepare Your
Students for
Math Workshop

This section explores best practices for preparing students for math workshop. It introduces the "three buckets" of setting up math workshop: classroom arrangement, routines and procedures, and mathematics community. It also offers twenty minilessons for establishing routines, procedures, and the community for math workshop to successfully happen. Implementing these lessons over the course of twenty days—and revisiting them as needed—helps ensure a successful math workshop.

. . . .

Chapters in Step 2

STEP 2

Twenty Days to a Classroom Culture That Works

Chapter 2

(continued)

The Three Buckets

It's helpful to tackle the setup of a classroom for math workshop via three categories or buckets. (See Table 2–1.) The three buckets represent the conditions that must be in place to ensure an effective and successful math workshop. When any one of these buckets is empty (left unattended), math workshop is difficult or nonexistent. What is left is either the traditional model of mathematics instruction or mass chaos.

Of course, classroom management systems, class sizes, and grade levels all impact how math workshop may look in any one classroom. Regardless of the variants, a classroom's physical space and culture should be set up in a way that allows for optimum facilitation of math workshop. How can this be done? Let's take some time to explore each of the three buckets in depth.

BUCKET	CATEGORY	DESCRIPTION
1	**Classroom Arrangement**	This bucket focuses on the ***where*** of math workshop. It is considered "full" when the physical setup of the classroom has been addressed. Is your space arranged to be as conducive as possible to math workshop? While you may not have the largest room or the newest resources, make the most of what you do have—it matters!
2	**Routines and Procedures**	This bucket focuses on ***how*** to make math workshop work. It is considered "full" when you have taken the appropriate steps to establish routines and procedures for math workshop. Do your students know what to expect?
3	**Mathematics Community**	This bucket focuses on both the ***how*** and the ***why***. It is considered "full" when a strong mathematics community has been established and is continually reinforced—one in which students are willing to take risks, communicate with one another, and be open to various perspectives.

Table 2–1. The three buckets representing the conditions that must be in place to ensure an effective and successful math workshop

Bucket 1: Classroom Arrangement

This bucket focuses on the *where* of math workshop. It is considered "full" when the physical setup of the classroom has been addressed. Is your space arranged to be as conducive as possible to math workshop? While you may not have the largest room or the newest resources, make the most of what you do have—it matters!

There are three key places to identify and create when arranging a classroom for math workshop:

1. A place to meet with the whole class (number sense routine and student reflection)

2. Appropriate places for students to meet in small groups (learning stations)

3. A place for the teacher to meet with a small group of students (guided math)

A place to meet with the whole class (number sense routine and student reflection) Students need to believe that they are a part of a learning community. Starting and ending each math workshop together as a whole group reinforces this belief. Whole-class discussions are a key time to ensure that students know they are responsible for their learning and feel accountable for the learning of their peers. In a math workshop, these whole-class meetings typically transpire at the beginning as part of a number sense routine (see Chapter 6 for an in-depth look at routines) and at the end as a reflection (see Chapter 9 for more on reflections). The ideal classroom arrangement for such may involve students sitting in a circle on a carpet or even seated at their desks in groups.

Appropriate places for students to meet in small groups (learning stations) Students, when working in learning stations, will often have at least one partner or might be in groups of three to four students. There is no one best way to set up a learning station—students might sit at adjoined desks, small tables, designated areas on the floor, computer centers, and more. What spaces in your room can serve as places for partner and small group work? Having all materials accessible for each station will help increase student time on task. Therefore, considering where you keep commonly used materials such as dice, blocks, and even extra paper and pencils can make students' work at learning stations more productive. Do be sure that there is little to distract students outside of their station—and more importantly, make sure each space is conducive to collaboration, communication (talk), critical thinking, and creativity.

A place for the teacher to meet with a small group of students (guided math)

In this book the term, *guided math* describes small-group instruction that happens during math workshop (see Chapter 8 for an in-depth look at guided math). It is one component of math workshop (just as guided reading is one component of reading workshop). Your guided math lessons will likely happen in a variety of places in the classroom. As you walk around the room observing students, you might simply pull a chair up to a group and help facilitate their thinking. However, you will also want to pull students to a designated area for small-group lessons. The area might be a table or an area on the floor. Take into account these two considerations as you arrange your small-group space:

1. Does the small-group area allow you to see what is going on in the rest of your classroom, especially at the learning stations?
2. Can the small-group area easily accommodate materials for students to work with (whiteboards, dry erase markers, paper and pencils, and a variety of manipulatives)?

Bucket 2: Routines and Procedures

This bucket focuses on *how* to make math workshop work. It is considered "full" when you have taken the appropriate steps to establish routines and procedures for math workshop. Do your students know what to expect?

A lot of time is spent in the beginning of a school year teaching students where to turn in their papers, how to line up for lunch, how to prepare for a fire drill, and so on. Time is also likely devoted to routines and procedures for reading and writing workshop. The time spent on these routines ensures that each day for the rest of the year runs smoothly. The same can be said for the routines and procedures for math workshop, especially as students participate in learning stations that are engaging activities for students to explore mathematical ideas. As teachers we shouldn't assume that students will automatically carry over routines and procedures they've learned for reading workshop to math workshop. We need to allot time to help students understand the expectations for math workshop. The minilessons provided in this chapter support the introduction of routines and procedures to students for math workshop.

For starters, when students are asked to engage in learning stations, they should easily and quickly know the answers to these questions:

- What can I do?
- Where do I go?
- Who can I work with?
- How long do I do it?
- What do I do if I have a question?
- What do I do when I'm finished?

What can I do? It is important that students are clear about what their options are for learning stations. Having a system for communicating this to them is imperative. In math workshop, we frequently call these systems *menus*. There is not one menu type that I necessarily like more than the other; it really depends on my students (see page 171 in Chapter 7 for some of my favorite menu ideas).

I recommend that as a teacher you give a menu enough time before you decide that it does or does not work for your class. Refrain from switching your menu each and every unit or week. Give students ample time to get used to it. Then, if you find that it is not working for you or your students, go ahead and choose another.

Chapter 7 goes into more detail about learning stations; the important things to consider when introducing these activities to students and establishing routines and procedures are that students must understand what the learning stations are, know how to interact with the station, and be clear about the expectations while engaging with the station.

Where do I go? Students need to know expectations for where they can work in their learning stations. Are you comfortable with them on the floor? Under desks? Do they need to stay where the station is located, or can they take the materials to another place in the room? These decisions vary from teacher to teacher, often influenced by students' behavior as well as the type and size of the classroom. I have tried both ends of the spectrum; in some math workshops, I've allowed students to sit anywhere. In others, I've defined where students are allowed to work.

In addition to where students go to work, they need to know where they go to get the necessary materials. This will save you many interruptions, especially if you are doing guided math groups. If you do not spend the time setting this up, your students are bound to interrupt your guided math group, asking questions like, "Where are the coins for the money activity?" It's also important to make sure students know where to find extra paper and pencils, additional manipulatives, or anything else that they may need in order to work independent of you.

Who can I work with? There may be times when you are completely comfortable having your students choose with whom they work—and other times you'll want to determine their partners. At times individual conversations may be necessary regarding who a student can and cannot work with if the student isn't showing healthy partner choices in learning stations. No matter who students work with, spend some time talking to students about how to work with one another and how to be a good "thinking partner" (the minilessons offered later in this chapter encourage characteristics of a good partner—actively listening, sharing, and more).

How long do I do it? Some learning stations may only take five minutes whereas others may take several days to complete. It is important that students know the expectations for how long they should remain at a station. When considering this question, I'm often asked about timed rotations—setting a time limit and having students move on to the next station when the time is up. See Chapter 7 for a discussion of the pros and cons of *timed rotations* versus the idea of *open station choice*.

What do I do if I have a question? Even if something has been explained numerous times, students inevitably have questions. Eric Jensen, an educational leader in the brain-based learning movement, once shared in a presentation something that has always resonated with me. He shared how frustrated he used to get when he was approached by a student two minutes after he gave the directions and the student would ask, "What are we supposed to do?" Then one day Jensen realized that instead of being frustrated, he could focus on the fact that the student was interested enough to ask—which was a lot better than a student who would choose to simply not do the activity. So now, whenever Jensen gets that question, he takes a deep breath, thanks the student for caring, and then gives the instructions again. Jensen's experience has in turn helped me as a teacher think about how to handle students' questions.

I've found it of most help to encourage students to first ask their classmates before coming to the teacher with a question. You might have seen the saying posted in classrooms—*Ask Three Before Me!*—which means ask three of your peers before coming to the teacher. This idea is great—just make sure it resides within a well-developed classroom community that encourages and supports students in asking questions of one another. For many students, being honest with their peers about their misconceptions or confusions can be intimidating.

> See Minilesson 14 in this chapter to help build a classroom culture conducive to asking questions.

What do I do when I'm finished? One of the biggest fears teachers have when starting learning stations is that students will waste valuable learning time. After all, the school day, and especially the math block, is already so short. I once had a student tasked with writing a story in writing workshop. I noticed that at one point she just stopped writing. When I approached her, she told me, completely straight-faced, that she was at the bottom of the paper and so she just could not write any more. With an amused smile, I explained to her that should this happen again, she should either get a new sheet of paper or turn the paper over and write on the back. She looked at me like I had just discovered the moon! Just like in reading and writing workshop, students during math workshop need to know what the expectations are for when they complete a station activity. Expectations may include:

- ideas for extending the activity;
- the best way to clean up the materials that were used, including putting materials back so that other students can experience the activity; and

- how to move quickly and efficiently to another station (it's especially important to practice and fine-tune transition times to maximize the learning time during math workshop—see Minilesson 12 in this chapter to support this).

See Minilesson 12 in this chapter to support moving quickly and efficiently from one station to another.

Reflect on It!

What routines and procedures do you already have in place? Which do you think are the most challenging for students to learn?

Bucket 3: Mathematics Community

This bucket focuses on both the *how* and the *why*. It is considered "full" when a strong mathematics community has been established and is continually reinforced—one in which students are willing to take risks, communicate with one another, and be open to various perspectives.

Community is a critical part of making math workshop work. Without community, students may struggle to work collaboratively, take risks, share their thinking, and feel comfortable being wrong in front of one another. The time that it takes to develop a strong community is well worth it! It's also important to note that developing this community is an ongoing process.

Reflect on It!

Imagine that you just walked into a mathematics class in which a community has not yet been established. What might you see happening? How does it make you feel? Now imagine that you've walked into a classroom with a strong mathematics community. What do you see? What do you hear? How does it make you feel? Compare your thinking to that in Table 2-1 (see page 40).

EVIDENCE OF A WEAK CLASSROOM COMMUNITY	EVIDENCE OF A STRONG CLASSROOM COMMUNITY
Students will not talk to one another; they keep their thinking to themselves.	Students talk to one another; they explain and clarify their thinking to each other.
Students see working together as cheating; they work alone.	Students see working together as learning; they collaborate, ask each other questions, and respectfully challenge ideas.
Students believe that they are either good at math or bad at math, and that this really can't change—they exhibit a fixed mindset.	Students believe that they are all capable of being successful in math—they exhibit a growth mindset.
Students are reluctant to struggle; instead they wait to be rescued by the teacher or by another student.	Students constructively struggle together and hold all members of the group accountable for learning.
Students are disrespectful of their peers' ideas.	Students respect their peers' ideas and view one another as knowledgeable.
Students hide their work from each other.	Students share their work with each other.
Students feel that their opinions and ideas *don't* matter—it's not worth the risk!	Students feel their opinions and ideas *do* matter—it's worth the risk!

Table 2–2. What makes a strong mathematics classroom community?

Developing a strong mathematics community takes a lot of thoughtful work. It's important to acknowledge that a mathematics community does not happen automatically just because students have an established reading and writing community. I've walked into classrooms during the reading and writing workshop and seen students engaged in amazing conversations about the books that they are reading—respectfully disagreeing with each other and openly sharing their opinions.

I was surprised to find that these same students, when observed during a math class—did the exact opposite. Rather than engage in respectful conversations, they tended to keep to themselves, hide their work, and struggle with explaining their ideas. When asked to talk to each other about a problem, students were quick to turn to their partners and say something like, "The answer is 23." The teacher, who was trying hard to get students to talk about their thinking, would then urge them to share their strategies and their thinking processes, not just the answer. The students would nod, then lean into their partners a second time and say something like, "I just added up the numbers." It became apparent that these students did not know how to discuss mathematics. While they could discuss their feelings about the plot of a book and disagree with the predictions made about a science experiment, they were not yet able to have these same rich conversations about mathematics.

In *From Reading to Math*, Maggie Siena (2009) suggests keeping four practices in mind when establishing a mathematics community:

1. Value thinking processes as well as correct answers.
2. Value problems for which more than one answer is possible.
3. Value inquisitive responses.
4. Value tolerance for mistakes.

So, how do we help students establish a community that supports these four practices and more? I suggest the following for starters:

- Model and encourage the use of talk moves.
- Model and encourage the use of sentence frames and starters.
- Encourage constructive struggling.
- Encourage the sharing of multiple strategies.

Model and encourage the use of talk moves
I find the guidance by Chapin, O'Connor, and Anderson in their *Talk Moves* (2013) video-based resources to be of immense help in establishing strong mathematics communities. I encourage educators to watch these videos of teachers and students using the talk moves and then focus on using the moves consistently in their own classrooms. When modeled correctly and embedded in the classroom culture, students will begin using talk moves with one another. It's a beautiful moment when you hear a student say to another, "Tell me more about. . . ." Consider posting talk moves in the classroom for students to continually reference. (See Figure 2–1 on the next page.)

For further ideas on introducing talk moves to students, see Minilesson 3 in this chapter.

Figure 2–1. Talk Moves poster (adapted from Chapin, O'Connor, and Anderson 2013; available at mathsolutions.com)

Model and encourage the use of sentence frames and starters I have found that sentence frames are highly successful in helping all students understand how to talk with one another during math workshop. Sentence frames have blanks that need to be completed in order to communicate an answer and/or strategy. For example, a learning station might task partners with drawing digit cards and comparing them. As part of the learning station there is a sentence frame that reads:

_____ is greater than _____.

This sentence frame supports students in knowing how to talk about the comparison of the two numbers.

At another station, students may be tasked with adding two numbers that have been rolled on two number cubes. The sentence frame in that station might read:

I rolled a _____ and a _____ , so I have _____.

In addition to sentence frames, sentence starters are also a wonderful way to encourage communication and build a mathematics community. Consider posting a list of starters in the classroom where all students can reference it as they work in their learning stations. The list might look something like the list in Figure 2–2 on the next page.

I agree with _____ because . . .
I would like to add on to what _____ said . . .
I respectfully disagree with _____ because . . .
Will you help me to understand _____?
Tell me more about _____.
I solved the problem by . . .
My first step was to . . .
This problem reminds me of . . .
What made you think to . . . ?
I wonder why . . .
I wonder if . . .

Figure 2–2. Sentence starters for use during math workshop

For further ideas on using sentence frames and starters with students, see Minilessons 3 and 4 in this chapter.

Sentence frames and sentence starters help a student articulate his or her thinking during a specific task or activity. Sentence starters also help to kick off a conversation. Both sentence frames and starters are invaluable in establishing a mathematics community. I recommend the series Supporting English Language Learners in Math Class written by Bresser and colleagues (2009), which includes video, for further insight into the use of sentence frames and starters.

Reflect on It!

What kinds of conversations are your students having in math class? How do you see the use of sentence frames and starters supporting math talk in your classroom?

Encourage constructive struggling   Seeley (2009) advocates for *constructive struggling*, a term that refers to the positive place students reach when presented with engaging and challenging problems. "As students engage in the constructive struggling needed for some of these problems, they learn that perseverance, in-depth analysis, and critical thinking are valued in mathematics as much as quick recall, direct skill application, and instant intuition" (90). This is first mentioned in Chapter 1 as a characteristic of defining math workshop.

To encourage and support constructive struggling in a math community, as teachers we must refrain from rescuing students when we see them struggle. When we make such "superhero" efforts, we reinforce the idea that the student cannot possibly be successful in mathematics without the support of the teacher. The underlying message is, "You can't do this on your own."

One might think, I'm not rescuing—I'm scaffolding. While there is a lot to be said for scaffolding, there is a fine line between scaffolding and rescuing. Take some time to identify where that line is and be conscientious of crossing it. It will likely be challenging at first; after all, we are teachers and we want to help students. However, in our efforts to walk a student through the steps or get them started, we may be "stealing" the opportunity from them to figure it out. Instead, encourage students to think of ways to get "unstuck" (see Minilesson 13 in this chapter). Make a commitment to let students struggle. In doing so they will learn self-reliance and perseverance—both important parts of a math community.

See Minilesson 13 in this chapter for ways to get students "unstuck."

Encourage the sharing of multiple strategies   A strong math community is one in which students see each other as valuable contributors and respect each other's ideas, opinions, and strategies. As teachers, we should create a culture in which multiple strategies are heard, honored, and discussed. We've all been there—we look up at the clock, realize we only have fifteen more minutes of class, and jump into rush mode to get through everything (after all, we are supposed to be moving on to a new topic by the end of the week!). Sometimes this means we stop at the first right answer we hear or, worse, give the answer and move on. The rush to get through it all often leaves us as teachers in conflict between coverage and understanding. The article, by Steven C. Reinhart, "Never Say Anything a Kid Can Say" (2000) is great for supporting why we need to slow down, talk less, and listen more.

One concern I often hear from teachers is that, by encouraging multiple strategies, students will lose sight of strategies that make the most sense and

For further ideas on supporting students in sharing multiple strategies, see Minilessons 5 and 15 in this chapter.

are the most efficient. However, with time, you will see that students can and will start to determine which strategy is most efficient in particular circumstances, just as experienced golfers determine which club to use and when (all the clubs are valuable, but a nine-iron may not help me on my first shot off the tee). Opportunities for determining efficiency can happen during focus lessons and guided math groups, in problems with more than one answer, and in problems with one answer but more than one entry point. See Chapter 5 for more details on ways to determine efficient strategies.

Twenty Minilessons

The last part of this chapter offers twenty minilessons for use in the first ten to fifteen minutes of each math class to prep students for math workshop. These lessons do not mean that you have to wait twenty days—and go through all twenty lessons—before starting math content. Rather, use these lessons as you start implementing math workshop. You can introduce a minilesson alongside mathematics content.

The current reality in education is that as teachers we have a lot to teach in a short period of time. It is not feasible to give up twenty full days of math instruction in order to prepare students for math workshop—and this is certainly not the intention of this section. These minilessons are intended to complement your math instruction, not replace it or postpone it. See Minilesson 20 for an understanding of how each minilesson can play out alongside the beginnings of math workshop. Remember, *Go Slow to Go Fast!*

See Minilesson 20 in this chapter for an understanding of putting all the lessons together.

These lessons focus on establishing routines, procedures, and the community needed for successful math workshop to happen. They ensure that the Buckets 2 and 3, routines and procedures and mathematics community, become and remain full throughout the year.

You might be familiar with *First 20 Days* for reading and writing workshop from Fountas and Pinnell's book *Guiding Readers and Writers, Grades 3–6* (2001) or *The Daily 5* from "The 2 Sisters," Gail Boushey and Joan Moser (2014). If so, you likely already know the value of taking the time to set your classroom up for success. Many of the same procedures discussed by these talented authors are beneficial in a math workshop setting.

Though each of these lessons should take no more than fifteen minutes a day, you may need to spend more time on some of them than others. You may also choose to mix up the order of these lessons based on what your math objective is for the day. And don't expect immediate results; after fifteen minutes of a lesson on writing about thinking, all of your students might not yet be able to write pages to describe their mathematical reasoning. These lessons are meant to be an introduction to your expectations, and you will most likely need to revisit these expectations throughout the year. Just remember, the end result is that your procedures are clear and students have had plenty of time to practice them prior to jumping into a full math workshop.

An Overview of the Twenty Minilessons

Use the following table to quickly locate a lesson as well as ensure that the anchor chart introduced in Minilesson 1 and labeled *Guidelines for Math Workshop* is appropriately created as you progress through the lessons. A play button ▶ indicates that the lesson includes a related video clip.

MINILESSON	LESSON TITLE	GUIDELINES FOR MATH WORKSHOP	DESCRIPTION
1	Being an Active Listener	I will be an active listener.	This lesson encourages students to think about the value of listening to one another—not just the teacher.
2	Making Connections	I will make connections between math and the world around me.	This lesson encourages students to look for connections in the real world, in previous problems, and with other content areas. While it may be challenging for younger students to identify where mathematics is used, they can certainly share where they see numbers in the real world.
3	Talking About Your Thinking ▶	I will talk about my thinking in math.	This lesson encourages students to start talking about math. Most of the time, you won't have a problem getting your students to talk. The key will be to get them to talk about mathematics!
4	Writing About Your Thinking	I will write about my thinking in math.	This lesson introduces students to the value of sentence frames and sentence starters in talking and writing about their thinking. For younger students, writing can be exhausting. Having short sentences for them to fill out or complete in a journal can help them to slowly build stamina. You can also encourage them to draw pictures of their thinking.
5	Using Your Strategies ▶	I will use different strategies to help me solve problems.	This lesson emphasizes the importance of students exploring mathematics and arriving at their own strategies. It's likely most appropriate for students in second grade and onward.
6	Working Collaboratively ▶	[see Minilesson 7]	This lesson emphasizes the importance of working together. Every student has an idea to share and should never be afraid to do so.

(continued)

MINILESSON	LESSON TITLE	GUIDELINES FOR MATH WORKSHOP	DESCRIPTION
7	Working Independently	I will do my best work whether working collaboratively or independently.	This lesson helps students understand that while they are a community of mathematicians who usually work together, there will be times that they need to work on their own.
8	Using Math Tools	[see Minilesson 9]	This lesson gets students thinking about the various tools they can use in math workshop. Tools such as rulers, compasses, and calculators are all very different. This can be confusing to students; discussing these differences and the purposes of the tools will help. Refer back to this lesson whenever a new tool is introduced.
9	Using Manipulatives	I will use math tools and manipulatives responsibly to help my thinking.	This lesson gives students the opportunity to start exploring math through manipulatives—an important part of the learning process. Refer back to this lesson whenever a new manipulative is introduced.
10	Representing Your Thinking	I will represent my thinking visually when helpful.	This lesson gives students the opportunity to explore the value of visual representations. Drawing pictures is an invaluable tool for helping students explain their thinking—even for older students! Refer back to this lesson if students get caught up in making the picture "pretty" rather than focusing on the mathematics.
11	Giving Your Best Effort	I will give my best effort and be respectful to my classmates.	This lesson encourages students to think about what it means to "give your best effort." Young children can all talk about working hard and making good choices. You may want to focus on this aspect of the lesson if you teach K–2. However, in grades 3–5, focus on accountability and what that looks like in the classroom.
12	Transitioning Between Activities	I will transition from one activity to the next quickly and without disrupting others.	This lesson helps students think about best practices when transitioning between learning stations. Revisit this lesson throughout the year to remind students of the importance of transitions—especially if you find materials left in a mess or if students are stopping to chat en route to their next station.

MINILESSON	LESSON TITLE	GUIDELINES FOR MATH WORKSHOP	DESCRIPTION
13	Getting Started or Getting Unstuck	I will help others get started and get unstuck as needed.	This lesson encourages students to think about what to do if they get stuck. Younger students may not need this lesson as much as older students (second grade and up) who tend to be more conscientious of making mistakes and asking questions. However, feel free to refer to this if you have a group of students who shoot up their hands and ask for help before they even attempt to get started.
14	Asking Questions	I will persevere through difficult math, never give up, and believe in myself.	This lesson helps students think about what makes a good question and learn how best, through perseverance, to handle questions they may have. Refer back to this lesson if you have a group of students who consistently turn to you as the teacher or immediately ask questions before giving themselves ample time to struggle at a learning station.
15	Exploring Math in Many Ways	I will explore math in more ways than one.	This lesson helps students think about the importance of exploring math in more than one way. Students understand that we may have different answers to questions like, "What is your favorite color?" or "What is your favorite food?"; however, many don't think that kind of flexibility exists in math. It is critical to do this lesson within the first twenty days of starting math workshop; however, it is even more important to remember to include tasks like this in the days that follow.
16	Checking Your Work	I will check my work.	This lesson focuses on best practices in checking one's own work. It is meant for older students (grade 3 and up). Younger students can still work on the skills of estimation and flexibility within the base ten number system.
17	Using Math Vocabulary	I will use ways to help me understand and remember new vocabulary.	This lesson provides ideas for how students can process new vocabulary; it is most appropriate for students in grade 3 and up.

(continued)

MINILESSON	LESSON TITLE	GUIDELINES FOR MATH WORKSHOP	DESCRIPTION
18	Reflecting and Sharing	I will reflect on my learning.	The lesson encourages students to see the value in reflecting on their learning. Reflection is so important that it is a key component of math workshop regardless of the structure. Remember, even very young mathematicians have brilliant ideas to share; don't be tempted to skip the reflection or this lesson just because your students are young.
19	Understanding the Guidelines for Math Workshop ▶	N/A [the chart is now complete; revisit the chart with students as needed]	This lesson is a culmination and review of the eighteen previous minilessons. Treat the chart that is created as a living document—one that can be revised as needed. As students engage in math workshop, they may want to clarify and/or add to some of the statements on the chart.
20	Putting It All Together	N/A	This lesson provides an example of how to use each of the above minilessons as part of starting your math workshop. If you haven't already, start math workshop—not with all of the components, but with a few (remember, Go Slow to Go Fast!). Each day you will build on the previous day, adding more choice, independence, and time for guided math groups. Don't worry—it will be great! And if it isn't, reflect on and identify what went wrong. Refer back to the minilessons here to help fine-tune the process.

Being an Active Listener

Overview

In this lesson, students consider the importance of active listening and practice being active listeners.

Many times we think we are listening, but our minds are wandering—we are thinking about and preparing our responses, thinking about questions we have, or thinking about how a comment applies to us. Being an active listener does not come naturally or easily; it is something that we have to work on and practice.

What is an "active listener"? An active listener is one who listens to another speaker while suspending judgment. Active listeners are not thinking about themselves, their comments, their work, their answers, or their questions. Active listeners are completely engaged in hearing the speaker and making sure to not be distracted.

> Students learn through sharing their ideas, listening to and critiquing the ideas of others, and by having others critique their approaches to solving problems.
>
> —Margaret S. Smith and Mary Kay Stein, authors of *5 Practices for Orchestrating Productive Mathematics Discussions* (2011)

Materials

None

Directions

You have probably all heard how important it is to listen in school. But many of you may think that only applies when you have to listen to the teacher. It is important to listen to what I say; however, it is equally important to listen to each other. Each of you has so many great ideas and wonderful questions. We can learn a lot from each other. But that means that when one of you is talking, everyone in the room is listening to what he or she is saying, not thinking about their own questions or about what they would like to share. We are going to practice this today, and we are going to work on this every single day in our classroom and in math workshop. Let's practice with this topic:

Would someone be willing to share a favorite way to spend a weekend?

(continued)

Select one student to share. Remind the other students that their job is to be an active listener. As the student finishes her description, use talk moves to ensure that the rest of the students have listened to what their classmate said. You might say:

- *Turn and talk to a shoulder partner about what _____ said about how she likes to spend the weekend.*
- *Who can repeat what _____ said about how she likes to spend the weekend?*
- *Tell me how _____ likes to spend the weekend, using your own words.*

At this point, help students understand that this is not a time to make connections to how they spend the weekend or to discuss if they do the same thing. A student may say that he likes to take his dog to the dog park, and the next thing you know, fifteen hands are going up.

- "I have a dog!"
- "I had a dog, but he died."
- "My grandfather's dog was brown."
- "My sister's friend has a dog and it smells."

As we all know, this can go on and on and completely derail a lesson. Should this happen, point out that these are ways to *connect* to what the speaker said, but that doing this is actually an example of *not* actively listening.

Ask students to reflect on why it is important to listen to one another and how they feel when someone does not listen to them. Ask students to share out ways that they will focus on being an active listener.

Anchor Chart

At the end of Minilesson 1, begin an anchor chart for students titled *Guidelines for Math Workshop*. Post the chart where every student can reference it throughout math workshop. You will be adding to this anchor chart each day as you progress through the twenty lessons. The first statement to list on this chart is:

I will be an active listener.

Making Connections

Overview

In this lesson, students think about the importance of making connections by brainstorming how math relates to the world around them.

Your students have probably heard a lot about making connections during reading. Making connections is also extremely helpful during math. When introduced to a mathematical concept, activity, or problem, it may be helpful to make a connection to real life or to another problem, activity, or previous concept. By understanding how math relates to other things, students make sense of numbers and have a greater understanding of the importance and relevance of math, no matter what they decide to do in the future.

> **Understanding is a measure of the quality and quantity of connections that a new idea has with existing ideas.**
>
> —John Van de Walle, Karen S. Karp, and Jennifer M. Bay–Williams, authors of *Elementary and Middle School Mathematics: Teaching Developmentally, Seventh Edition* (2010)

Materials

- notebook paper for each student

Directions

Give each student several pieces of notebook paper.

You have already been making connections during reading; today we are going to talk about how making connections in math can help you learn. Sometimes you can make a connection to real life or to another problem, activity, or concept that you have seen in the past.

Let's take a moment to brainstorm how math relates to the world around us. You may choose anything that you have ever learned in math. On a piece of paper, write down a concept and its connection to the real world. For example, the connection that I'm writing down is:

(continued)

> *I put gas in my car this morning. The gas cost $3.20 per gallon. I knew that if I needed to put 10 gallons of gas in my car, I would spend over $30. Putting gas in my car is related to money and estimation.*

Give each student time to write several ideas down, one per piece of paper. Have students crumple up their notes and place them in a bag or other container. Pull the ideas out of the bowl, one by one, and read them to the class. No student names are attached to the notes; therefore, this structure is low risk.

Younger students may have an easier time with this activity if they are asked to think about where they see math in their life. Examples might include numbers on mailboxes, their parents' cell phone numbers, money, or a clock. You could also ask them to think of a special number and tell why it is special. For example:

- "Three is special because there are three kids in my family."
- "Ten is special because my birthday is on the 10th of January."

Anchor Chart

Add to your *Guidelines for Math Workshop* anchor chart:

I will make connections between math and the world around me.

Talking About Your Thinking

Overview

In this lesson students think about the importance of respectful communication in math and practice talking about their mathematical reasoning.

No longer is math class a place where students should be quietly working alone on a problem. While there may be times that you want your students to not talk so everyone can think to themselves, communication should be a normal part of a math lesson—and math workshop. Encourage students to discuss their thinking regularly with one another, either in pairs or with the whole class, throughout math class. Some students may be more comfortable taking this risk than others. It is important to discuss how to help everyone feel comfortable talking. Students need to know that each of their classmates have ideas and opinions; respecting everyone's ideas is imperative, and being open-minded to others' ideas will make everyone a better learner.

> **When teachers commit themselves to *teaching for understanding*, classroom discourse and discussion are key elements in the overall picture.**
>
> —Suzanne H. Chapin, Catherine O'Connor, Nancy Canavan Anderson, authors of *Talk Moves, Third Edition* (2013)

According to *Number Talks* author Sherry Parrish, "[There are] benefits of sharing and discussing computation strategies. Students have the opportunity to

1. clarify their own thinking;
2. consider and test other strategies to see if they are mathematically logical;
3. investigate and apply mathematical relationships;
4. build a repertoire of efficient strategies; and
5. make decisions about choosing efficient strategies for specific problems. (2010, 11)

Materials

- an open-ended math problem (see suggestions at the end of this lesson)
- sentence frames and starters (see suggestions at the end of this lesson)

(continued)

Directions

You are all knowledgeable students with wonderful ideas. It is important that we take the time to learn from one another. Some of us think best when we are able to process our thoughts out loud. Others do our best thinking when we have silent time first. There are times that I will encourage you to talk, and times that I will encourage you to think silently first. When we talk, it will be as a whole class, in small groups, or with a partner. Some of you may be more comfortable taking this risk than others. It is important that we discuss how to help everyone with this. We need to value everyone's thoughts and opinions. We need to be respectful of everyone's ideas; being open-minded to others' ideas will actually make us better learners.

Let's practice! At your table, you have a problem to solve. First, solve this problem independently and then allow each member of your group to talk, sharing how they solved it the way they did. Help each member of your group by encouraging them to discuss their strategies in detail and reminding them to be respectful of different answers or methods. Use the sentence frames posted to help you as you discuss this problem.

As students work together, it will be important to use *Talk Moves* (see page 41 in this chapter) to help them understand how to discuss this problem with one another. Consider asking questions that would help shape the conversations such as:

Can you explain _____'s strategy?

Can you add on to what _____ said?

Do you agree or disagree with _____'s answer?

It's important to remember that it takes a lot of practice for students to feel comfortable sharing and discussing their strategies. This is the start of an important process that will continue on a daily basis.

SUGGESTED PROBLEMS FROM SULLIVAN AND LILBURN (2002)

Grades K–2

- What numbers can you make using the digits 6, 5, and 8?
- How many different rectangles can you make using 12 square tiles?

Grades 3–4

- How many ways can you rename 1,265 as the sum of smaller numbers?
- I have $36 in my pocket. What bills and coins might I have?

Grade 5

- I doubled a number and kept doubling so that the original number was doubled 4 times. What might the answer be?

SUGGESTED SENTENCE FRAMES AND STARTERS

You might consider making sentence frames designed specifically for the problem that is being solved. For example, you might have a sentence frame for the first grade K–2 problem listed above that looks like this: *I used 6, 5, and 8 to make the number* _____. You could also make sentence frames and starters that are more generic such as:

I agree with _____'s strategy.

I thought about it a different way . . .

I disagree with _____ because _____.

 **VIDEO CLIP 2.1**

Talking About Your Thinking

In this clip, a team of fifth graders is engaged in a learning station activity, Toss 'n Talk, as part of math workshop. Students roll a sum, then they have to find the fraction equation that matches it. As you watch this clip, consider the following questions:

- What are the students doing to cultivate a culture of "talking about your thinking"?
- How are their interactions similar to or different from other student collaborations you've observed?

To view this video clip, scan the QR code or access via mathsolutions.com/mathworkshop21

Writing About Your Thinking

Overview

In this lesson students think about the importance of writing in math and practice writing about their mathematical reasoning.

Just as talking about thinking is an important component of learning, so is writing about thinking. When students write about the mathematical process before they work on the problem, during their work on the problem, and after their work (as a form of reflection), their thinking becomes clearer to the teacher and to themselves. Writing not only helps students make sense of numbers, strategies, and procedures; it also allows time to process and make connections.

> Writing can help students think more deeply and clearly about math because it requires students to organize, clarify, and reflect on their ideas—all useful processes for making sense of mathematics.
>
> —Marilyn Burns, author of *About Teaching Mathematics, Fourth Edition* (2015)

Each student should have a math journal—a place to record his or her thoughts. Students may choose to write down the steps they use to solve a problem, write about the solution in their own words, and/or reflect on what they learned in solving the problem. For younger students, writing can be exhausting. Having sentence frames and starters—short sentences for them to fill out or complete in a journal—can help them to slowly build stamina. Additionally, encourage younger writers to use pictures to represent their thinking.

Materials

- math journal, one per student (if you do not use math journals, a notebook or paper will work)
- math problem (see sample problems at the end of this lesson)
- sentence frames and starters

Directions

You each have your own math journal. You will use your journal this year to write about your thinking, record strategies that you use, and record strategies that you see your friends use. Recording your thinking helps you make sense out of numbers. You can use your journal to write down your steps in solving a problem, write about the problem and your thinking in your own words, and reflect on your learning. Writing about your thinking will help move you forward mathematically.

Let's practice writing about our math thinking using our math journals. At your table you will find a math activity or problem. You may work on this independently or collaboratively.

Present each group of students with a math activity or problem. Tell students that they may work on this independently or collaboratively.

- *Before:* Ask students to write down what strategy they think they will use to help them solve the problem. Then ask them to write down any connections they may have to this problem.

- *During:* As they work, ask students to focus on writing down the steps that they are taking and why they are taking them. Have them write about their new math learning.

- *After:* After they have completed the task, have students reflect on how this activity has changed the way they think or confirmed how they were thinking.

SAMPLE PROBLEMS

- Joey and his 3 friends Ray, Sean, and Naveen are standing in line at school. Joey isn't first. Sean isn't last. What are all the ways that the boys could be lined up?

- Lila went shopping for new socks. The first store had a pack of 10 pairs of socks listed for $32. The second store had a *Buy 1, Get 1 Free* special with each pair of socks costing $5.75. The third store had a pack of 8 pairs of socks listed for $35, and Lila had a coupon for 10% off. Which store should Lila buy her socks from and why?

Anchor Chart

Add to your *Guidelines for Math Workshop* anchor chart:

I will write about my thinking in math.

Using Your Strategies

Overview

In this lesson students become familiar with multiple strategies in solving math, explore strategies through solving a problem, and arrive at their own strategies.

When I was in school, I was typically taught a mathematical skill, then I practiced that skill on a worksheet of twenty-five problems, then I applied that skill to a couple of word problems at the bottom of the worksheet. This was the extent of my "problem solving." In today's classroom, teaching and learning math now happens *through* problem solving.

> **For students to learn mathematics with understanding, they must have opportunities to engage on a regular basis with tasks that focus on reasoning and problem solving and make possible multiple entry points and varied solution strategies.**
>
> —NCTM, *Principles to Actions: Ensuring Mathematics Success for All* (2014)

There are many problem-solving strategies that students can use. You may have already introduced students to problem-solving strategies. If not, some of the strategies listed by Van de Walle in *Elementary and Middle School Mathematics: Teaching Developmentally* (2010) include:

- Act It Out, Draw a Picture, Use a Model
- Look for a Pattern
- Make a Table or Chart
- Try a Simpler Form of the Problem
- Guess and Check
- Make a List

Consider posting a list of strategies—a *Problem-Solving Strategy* chart—where everyone can see it and refer to it as they solve problems.

Remember that the strategy that makes sense to one student may not be the strategy that makes sense to another. One student may choose to use a model, while another may choose to make a table. As teachers we need to send the message that a variety of strategies are encouraged and students should do what makes sense to them. We should also keep in mind that students learning strategies from each other is much more powerful than a teacher showing students a strategy. We must remember to not take the problem solving out of the problems we give to students by telling them which strategy to choose. Rather, we pose problems that lend themselves to a strategy we want them to develop (Van de Walle, Karp, and Bay-Williams, 2010).

Return to this lesson each time you see a notable strategy present in a student's work during math workshop. Showcasing how two students can both get the same answer with different strategies encourages the understanding of the strategies, promotes a respectful mathematics community, and helps students make connections across different mathematical ideas.

Materials
- math problem (see sample problems at the end of this lesson)
- *Problem-Solving Strategy* chart (posted in classroom)

Directions
It is important to become familiar with problem-solving strategies so that you can determine which to use for a particular problem. Some of the problem-solving strategies that we may use this year are on our strategy chart posted at the front of the classroom.

There are times that you will know how to solve a problem immediately. However, sometimes, you may be unsure. In those cases, using one of the strategies listed on the chart may help you.

You will get a chance to see many strategies this year. You may choose to use a strategy that is different from your classmates. In fact, everyone in your group may choose to use a different strategy, and yet, you could all solve the problem correctly! In this class, we respect one another and the different thinking that we have. It is our job as mathematicians to try to understand our classmates' strategies and encourage each other in the process.

Have students solve a math problem. Ask students to identify which strategies listed on the *Problem-Solving Strategy* chart are evident in each other's work.

Hold a class discussion. Be open to adding to the class strategy chart if students name a strategy that isn't already listed.

(continued)

SAMPLE PROBLEMS

- Two children have 3 brownies to share equally. How much brownie will each child get?

- There are 8 children on Coach Kerry's swim team. Each child is getting half of a sandwich. How many whole sandwiches will be needed?

- Rachel is having friends over for a party. There will be 5 children in all at the party. Each child wants 3 slices of pizza. How many whole pizzas will be needed? How will the pizzas be cut into fractional parts?

▶ VIDEO CLIP 2.2

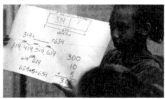

Sharing Strategies

In this clip Ms. Hrabak, as part of math workshop with fourth graders, facilitates a discussion on strategies used to solve the problem, *Jamie's family visited their grandmother, who lives 634 miles from their house. On the first day, they drove 319 miles. How many miles did they have left to drive the second day?* As you watch this clip, consider the following questions:

- Who are the strategies coming from and how?
- What message(s) is the teacher sending students about the use of strategies?

To see how the rest of Ms. Hrabak's math workshop unfolds around this strategy sharing excerpt, see Video Clip 4.1.

To view this video clip, scan the QR code or access via mathsolutions.com/mathworkshop22

Working Collaboratively

Overview

In this lesson students practice working together on a math problem and reflect on the importance of such.

Students need opportunities to work together—in math workshop this is essential. Working together helps students clarify their thinking, share their thought process, respect others' thinking, deepen their understanding, stay focused, and justify math solutions or strategies. Working together exposes students to other methods of solving a problem or other solutions to a problem. Seeing things from a different perspective may even be the catalyst in a student's math learning. By giving opportunities for students to work together, you are also promoting teamwork and encouraging math discourse.

> Giving students opportunities to voice their ideas helps them strengthen, extend, and cement their learning. To this end, it's valuable to make student interaction an integral part of instruction.
>
> —Marilyn Burns, author of *About Teaching Mathematics, Fourth Edition* (2015)

Materials

- *Working Collaboratively* chart (created in this lesson)
- sticky notes for each student
- an open-ended math problem (select a problem that corresponds with the math topic students are currently learning. A great resource to consider is *50 Problem-Solving Lessons, Grades 1–6* by Marilyn Burns (1996).

Directions

There will be many times during math workshop when I ask you to work with a partner or work with a small group. This is called collaboration. When you work collaboratively, I have some expectations so that our best learning can take place. Let's work together to create a chart about what collaborative learning will look like in our classroom. What expectations can we agree on that will help each of us learn best as we work together?

(continued)

Have students brainstorm together and write each of their thoughts on a separate sticky note. Then have them share their thoughts and either "stick" them to the chart, or you can write them on the chart directly. (See Figure 2–3.) If you are writing their ideas down, phrase the ideas in a positive way (e.g., "Talk respectfully" rather than "Don't talk mean").

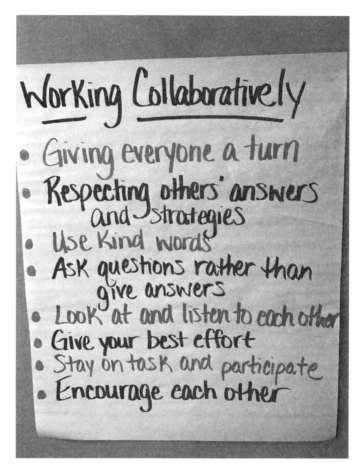

Figure 2–3. Sample of a Working Collaboratively chart

We may want to talk as a class about what to do if you have chosen a partner and realize you are unable to work with him or her. In some cases, you may find that it isn't always best to work with a friend. There are times when it may be appropriate to politely change partners, choosing a better fit. However, I hope that most of the time you will find a way to respectfully collaborate with your partner and progress through the task.

Now, let's take a moment to practice our expectations by working collaboratively on the following problem. Remember to refer to the chart if you or someone in your group is not following the expectations that we have listed.

At the end of the day's lesson, ask students to reflect on their work together.

Take a look at the chart that we made at the beginning of the class. Think about how your partners and you worked to solve problems today. Share an example of how one of your partners followed the expectations listed on our chart. Is there anything that we need to add to our chart to help us to collaborate better?

 **VIDEO CLIP 2.3** ·

Working Cooperatively

In this clip, Ms. Lempp facilitates a discussion with first grad-ers on "working cooperatively" as part of preparing them for math workshop. As you watch this clip, consider the following questions:

- How does the teacher phrase students' ideas in a positive way?
- How do you address the idea of working cooperatively in your classroom?

To view this video clip, scan the QR code or access via mathsolutions.com/mathworkshop23

Working Independently

Overview

In this lesson students practice working independently on a math problem and reflect on the importance of such.

While students' thinking and reasoning can become clear during discussion, it is necessary to prepare students for times when they will need to work on math independently. During independent work time, students show respect for others' thinking by working quietly. Through practiced independent work, students gain confidence in their own math ability. When the time comes for them to share their own thinking with others, they will feel like valued members of the group.

> Being able to see your work gives me a way to see if I was successful in teaching you, and what else I might need to do to be helpful.
>
> —Marilyn Burns, author of *About Teaching Mathematics, Fourth Edition* (2015)

Materials

- *Working Independently* chart (created during this lesson)
- open-ended word problems (see Minilesson 15 for sample problems)

Description

Yesterday we talked about how to work collaboratively. However, there will be times when you will need to work independently in math class. Working independently means that you are working by yourself and what you are working on will consist of your own thoughts—not the thoughts of others. This is often a way for me to collect data on how to help you best. So it is important to be honest about your knowledge and try your very best. Think about times that you have had to work independently. What might working independently look like? What are some ways that you ensured that your own thinking was represented on the task? How might others be acting so that you can work independently?

Have students independently brainstorm ideas, then share one idea with a partner. Partners share each other's ideas, not their own. Then record students' ideas on a *Working Independently* chart. Ideas might include:

- I will stay on task.

- I will do my best.

- I will be respectful of those around me.

Now, let's take a moment to practice our rules for independent work in math by solving the following problem. Remember to refer to the chart. Focus on just you and your thinking.

Share an open-ended word problem for students to solve.

Once students complete the problem, ask students to reflect on what was helpful to them about the time they were given to work independently. What helped them do their best thinking? Is there anything that we should add to the chart to help us to work independently?

Anchor Chart

Add to your *Guidelines for Math Workshop* anchor chart:

I will do my best work whether working collaboratively or independently.

Using Math Tools

Overview

In this lesson students are given the opportunity to discuss the various tools they might use in math workshop.

Understanding the use of tools is a valuable part of mathematical thinking; this is emphasized in the fifth Common Core State Standards for Mathematical Practice, which reads "Use appropriate tools strategically" (corestandards.org/Math/Practice/#CCSS.Math.Practice.MP5). Unfortunately, students may not use tools strategically, efficiently, or effectively without an appropriate introduction to them.

> **Meaning does not reside in tools; it is constructed by students as they use tools.**
>
> —James Hiebert, Thomas P. Carpenter, Elizabeth Fennema, Karen C. Fuson, Diana Wearne, Hanlie Murray, Alwyn Oliver, Piet Human, authors of *Making Sense: Teaching and Learning Mathematics with Understanding* (1997)

If I had a penny for every time I saw a student type a division problem into a calculator incorrectly, I'd be quite wealthy! The problem $4\overline{)604}$ gets typed into the computer $4 \div 604$ more often than I can count. And many students become very confused by the decimal point on the calculator; it's important to explain such.

As teachers, we need to remember that providing a student with a calculator or a ruler does not mean that they know *how* to use them. This lesson provides an opportunity for students to get to know these tools, recognize the differences in them, explore the tools just as students explore a math concept, and determine when they would be useful. Refer back to this lesson each time that a new tool is introduced.

Materials

- collection of calculators, rulers, protractors, compass, multiplication chart, and any other grade-level-appropriate tools

Directions

Whether you are working collaboratively or independently, you may need to use tools to help you with math. A math tool could be a calculator, ruler, protractor, and so on. It is important that we talk about how we use these tools. While today we will look at one or two tools, there are many more tools that you might find helpful as you think about math throughout the year.

Let's think about how a ruler and calculator can be helpful to us in math. Tell your partner about the value of these two tools. What are some things that we need to remember and think about when using these tools? For example, are all rulers the same? All calculators? Is the answer on the calculator always going to be correct? How will we know?

Ask students to share with a partner about a time that they used a tool to help them in mathematics.

Using Manipulatives

Overview

In this lesson students are given the opportunity to explore manipulatives they might use in math workshop. For the purpose of this book, I'm dealing with tools and manipulatives separately, as tools are often items that are used for a specific purpose (e.g., ruler to measure length, protractor to draw/measure an angle) and I'm advocating for manipulatives to be available for students in many if not all settings. Manipulatives, therefore, are items that will help support a student's thinking.

> Ideas exist in children's minds, and manipulatives help them construct an understanding of ideas that they can then connect to mathematical vocabulary and symbols.
>
> —Marilyn Burns, founder of Math Solutions

Manipulatives allow an abstract math concept to be represented in a concrete way. They include blocks, connecting cubes, and geoboards. Manipulatives can be even better than a picture because they are 3D. For students who need to touch and feel to learn best, manipulatives are often their "go-to" choice for working out a problem. Manipulatives are helpful for students of all ages and should be used in elementary, middle, and high school years. Just like with tools (see Minilesson 8), students need time to explore manipulatives before using them as part of learning.

Don't be tempted to show students exactly what to do with manipulatives or even which manipulatives to use in a certain situation. If you take out cubes and show students how to line them up to compare two quantities, then you have taught students a procedure rather than allowing them the opportunity to explore. Van de Walle and colleagues in *Elementary and Middle School Mathematics: Teaching Developmentally*, warn us that, "A natural result of overly directing the use of models is that children begin to use them as answer-getting devices rather than as tools used to explore a concept" (2010, 29).

Refer back to this lesson each time a new manipulative is introduced.

Materials

- collection of blocks, dice, connecting cubes, geoboards, cards, and any other grade-level-appropriate manipulatives

Directions

What are some math manipulatives that you have used in the past? The purpose of math manipulatives is the same as the purpose of a picture. It is to create a visual representation of a mathematical concept. There are times that manipulatives will not be needed. However, there are times that manipulatives can support our mathematical thinking.

It is often tempting to "play" with manipulatives rather than use them for learning. It is important to use manipulatives responsibly in order for them to help you learn. Therefore, let's take time to investigate some of the math manipulatives that we will be using often this year. I hope that this exploration will ensure that when we use them in class, you will be ready to use them properly. They are not toys.

Please take the next five minutes (adjust time to fit the needs of your class) *to explore the manipulatives that have been placed at your table. As you explore each manipulative, think about what it looks like, feels like and what it can do to help you. Have you ever used something like this before? If so, when and how?*

Once students have had an opportunity to explore, ask them to share with the group what they noticed about the manipulatives and how they might use them in the future.

Anchor Chart

Add to your *Guidelines for Math Workshop* anchor chart:

I will use math tools and manipulatives responsibly to help my thinking.

 **VIDEO CLIP 2.4**

Using Manipulatives

In this clip, Ms. Lempp gives kindergartners an opportunity to explore manipulatives they might use in math workshop. As you watch this clip, consider the following questions:

- Why does the teacher intentionally not give a mathematics task to students during this time?
- What does the teacher do to encourage students to share their thinking?

To view this video clip, scan the QR code or access via mathsolutions.com/mathworkshop24

Representing Your Thinking

Overview

In this lesson students are given the opportunity to explore the value of visual representations.

We've all likely heard the saying, "A picture is worth a thousand words." Pictures can help move students from concrete to abstract thinking. They are also a wonderful method of communicating steps and strategies, and an alternative to the use of manipulatives. Students don't need to be artists to draw pictures in math to help them learn, solve, and justify.

Refer back to this lesson if students get caught up in making the picture "pretty" rather than focusing on the mathematics.

> Visual representations help students to advance their understanding of mathematical concepts and procedures, make sense of problems, and engage in mathematical discourse.
>
> —NCTM, from *Principles to Actions: Ensuring Mathematical Success for All* (2014)

Materials

- paper, both blank and lined
- pencils, both colored and regular
- math problem (see sample problems at the end of this lesson)

Directions

We know that drawing a picture is one of our problem-solving strategies. It is a great method to help us process our thinking. Sometimes drawing pictures to help represent our math thinking will help us make sense of the numbers. Pictures can represent numbers, and pictures can help make sense out of a mathematical process. Pictures can take the place of words in math notes, and pictures can help us visualize a math concept best. Think about a time that something didn't make sense to you until you could see it. Share this with your partner.

Mathematicians draw pictures differently than artists draw pictures. For example, an artist may draw a book like this:

However, as mathematicians, we want to spend time thinking about our strategy rather than making a pretty picture of it. So, a mathematician may draw something like this to represent a book:

Today, as we learn about _____, practice drawing pictures to represent your math thinking. The pictures you draw might help you remember this concept in the future.

Share a problem with students and have them draw pictures to represent their mathematical thinking with the problem. Encourage students to post their thinking in the classroom. Have students circulate, thinking about what their peers did.

SAMPLE PROBLEMS

Grades K–2

- Half of the people in a family are males. What might a drawing of the family look like?

- You see a sign in a shop window that reads "$\frac{1}{2}$ off sale." What does this mean to you?

(continued)

Grades 3—4

- How many different designs can you make that are $\frac{3}{4}$ red and $\frac{1}{4}$ yellow?
- One-third of a class orders lunches from the cafeteria each day. How many students might be in the class and how many of them order lunches each day?

Grade 5

- A rectangle has a perimeter of twelve units. What might the area be?
- Write some different stories and draw visuals that might be represented by the equation: $3 \div \frac{1}{2}$.

Giving Your Best Effort

Overview

In this lesson students think about what it means to "give your best effort."

Young children can talk about working hard and making good choices. You may want to focus on this aspect of the lesson if you teach K–2. However, in grades 3–5, you should also focus on accountability and what that looks like in the classroom.

It is challenging for students to follow directions and make good choices 100 percent of the time—in fact, it's even difficult for adults! One of the biggest hurdles for teachers in math workshop tends to be the concern about accountability. As teachers we might worry, "How do I know that students are doing what they need to be doing over there, if I'm with these students over here?" The answer, which might be hard to hear, is this: sometimes students *won't* be doing what they are supposed to be doing, regardless of how well you've set up your math workshop. However, if you create a classroom culture where learning is at the forefront, students respect one another and themselves, risk taking is encouraged, and activities are differentiated and engaging, then most students will be doing the right thing; they will be accountable for their work.

If the concern is in defense of why students should only be taught as a whole class, then I ask, "How do you know anyone is paying attention to what you are saying in front of the room for sixty minutes?"

> The key to successful grouping is *individual accountability*. That means that while the group is working together on a product, each individual must be able to explain the process, the content, and the product.
>
> —John Van de Walle, Karen S. Kemp, and Jennifer M. Bay-Williams, authors of *Elementary and Middle School Mathematics, Seventh Edition* (2010)

Materials

- math journal, one per student (if you do not use math journals, a notebook or paper will work)

(continued)

Directions

When we are in math workshop, I may be working with small groups. During that time, I need to know that you are working as hard as you can in learning stations. You will need to use your time wisely and be respectful of those around you. If you are working with another student or a group, then your group members are counting on you, too! We all need to make the most out of every minute that we have of math workshop. Today, after each of the activities, I will ask you to share how you showed good effort and were accountable for your work. This may look different for each of you based on what you were working on.

Introduce the following method for students to rate their own effort on a scale of 0 to 5: students use their fists to indicate zero (meaning no effort at all), raise one finger to indicate one (meaning meager effort), and so on, with all five fingers raised indicating the best effort that they could give.

During all parts of the math workshop, you should be able to proudly and honestly say that you are working at your own personal level of 4 to 5. Brainstorm in small groups about what behaviors would be considered a 0, 1, 2, 3, 4, and 5.

Once students have worked in small groups, bring them back together as a whole class to share their thinking.

Following the math activities for the day, have students write to you about how they stayed accountable for their work, even if there was nothing to turn in to you. Ask them to rate themselves as a 0, 1, 2, 3, 4, and 5 and then explain why.

Anchor Chart

Add to your *Guidelines for Math Workshop* anchor chart:

I will give my best effort and be respectful of my classmates.

Transitioning Between Activities

Overview

In this lesson students think about best practices when transitioning between learning stations.

Transitions abound in our classrooms; students transition in and out of the room due to specials, lunch, and recess; to and from the restroom; between subjects; and between activities within the same subject. It's no wonder transitions consume a big amount of instructional time. In fact, if just 10 minutes of math class is spent on transitions and there are 180 school days a year, then 1,800 minutes per school year—or thirty hours—are being used on transitions. If your math class is one hour, then this is like being absent for 30 days! It is important for both teachers and students to be aware of how time on transitions adds up—and why it's important to make transitions as efficient as possible.

> **What's important is that students know what to do when they finish their work and that they continue to be involved in mathematical explorations throughout the time designated for mathematics.**
>
> —Linda Dacey, Jayne Bamford Lynch, and Rebeka Eston Salemi, authors of *How to Differentiate Your Math Instruction* (2013)

Revisit this lesson throughout the year to remind students of the importance of transitions—especially if you find students are stopping to chat en route to their next station or struggling to make their next station choice quickly.

Materials

- timer or timer tool
- math games (choose games that will not take too long and use materials). Consider *Math Games for Number and Operations and Algebraic Thinking* (Petersen 2013) as a source for ideas.

Directions

We are creating a mathematics classroom that ensures that each of you have the best opportunity to learn. It is important that we always challenge ourselves and also respect the learning of others. In order for our system to work best for math workshop and for us to get the most out of our math time, it is important that everyone spend as little

(continued)

time as possible transitioning from one activity to another. Transitions should be smooth and quick. This means that when you stop one activity, you clean up your materials and return them the way you found them. You quickly gather any materials needed for your next activity and get started immediately. Wasted time adds up, and over the course of a year, a lot of math learning time can be lost because of transitions.

Let's practice transitioning from one activity to another. Each group has one activity. Work on this activity for about ____ minutes (predetermine the time). When I give you the signal, clean up the materials, return them, and gather your materials for the next activity.

Use a timer or timer tool to help students understand how long it takes them to transition from one activity to another. These steps can be repeated several times with various activities. You may want to try to "challenge" students to see if they can beat their previous time.

On average, it took our class about ____ minutes to transition from one activity to the next. While speed is important, I also want you to remember that it is equally important to be safe and respectful of materials and of each other. We need to walk, not run, when we move from station to station, and we need to make sure that no materials are left behind.

While all transitions are not going to be timed in this manner and many of our transitions will be happening at different times when we fully implement math workshop, I hope that this lesson allows you to realize the expectations that we have when it comes to transitions in the classroom. Please discuss with your partner at least one way that we can all help to decrease the transition time while still being safe.

Ask for a few students to share ideas that they discussed with their partner.

Anchor Chart

Add to your *Guidelines for Math Workshop* anchor chart:

I will transition from one activity to the next quickly and without disrupting others.

Getting Started or Getting Unstuck

Overview

This lesson encourages students to think about what to do if they get stuck.

Sometimes as teachers we may feel that students need us to be there to walk them through a math problem step-by-step or answer every one of their questions. We may even feel that we are doing them harm by *not* taking these actions. However, as emphasized earlier in this resource, we should allow students to struggle at times.

> Sometimes mathematics is hard, and sometimes we have to struggle to figure things out, especially with problems that are complex.
>
> —Cathy L. Seeley, author of *Faster Isn't Smarter* (2009)

It is good for students to think about how they can get started and/or get unstuck—whether it means looking for other strategies on their own, talking to their peers, or making a connection to a similar problem that they have seen in the past.

When a student is stuck, instead of providing the answer, get into the habit of asking questions.

Younger students may not need this lesson as much as older students (second grade and up) who tend to be more conscientious of making mistakes and asking questions. However, feel free to refer to this if you have a group of students who shoot up their hands and ask for help before they even attempt to get started.

Materials

- *Problem-Solving Strategy* chart (see Minilesson 5)

Directions

We've talked about giving your best effort and making good choices when you are working. Sometimes it may be tough to get started, especially if the math activity is challenging. You may also get "stuck" and feel that you don't know how to move forward. Think of a time when you've had trouble getting started. How did you feel?

Sometimes getting started may be scary because you are afraid to be wrong. However, I believe that we learn as much from incorrect answers or methods as we do correct ones. I think that sometimes it is better to get started the "wrong way" than to never

(continued)

get started at all. Remember also that there are more mathematicians than you in this classroom. When you need assistance or need to talk something out, you are not alone. With your partner, discuss some things that you might do when you feel stuck.

After students have finished sharing with their partners, ask them to share their ideas with the whole class. Some of the ideas they may generate for getting unstuck include:

- make a connection to a similar problem you have solved in the past;

- refer to your *Problem-Solving Strategy* chart; or

- talk to another person about your thinking.

When students are stuck, instead of providing the answer, encourage students to think about questions like the following:

- What am I thinking?

- What do I know? Understand?

- Does this problem remind me of a problem I have previously solved? If so, what?

- What am I being asked to do in this problem?

It is important to remember our problem-solving strategies; they can come in handy when we don't know how to solve something. Let's take a look at our problem-solving strategies and keep these in mind when we are struggling with a problem or activity. Tomorrow we will talk about how to ask for help and/or ask questions.

Revisit the *Problem-Solving Strategy* chart created in Minilesson 5.

Anchor Chart

Add to your *Guidelines for Math Workshop* anchor chart:

I will help others get started and get unstuck as needed.

Asking Questions

Overview

In this lesson students think about what makes a good question—and learn how best to handle questions they may have.

We all know that kids have questions—a lot of them! It is important to have a system for handling questions in our classrooms. As teachers we want to promote an environment where students feel free to ask questions, challenge one another, and look for justification of answers. However, some questions, like, "What do I do when I'm done?" can be a distraction, especially during math workshop.

> **Allowing students to collaborate on tasks provides support and challenge for students, increasing their chance to communicate about mathematics and build understanding.**
>
> —John Van de Walle, Karen S. Karp, and Jennifer M. Bay-Williams, authors of *Elementary and Middle School Mathematics*, Seventh Edition (2010)

Be proactive about creating a system for handling questions. Tell students that you appreciate good questions that really make everyone think harder about math. However, interrupting you during math workshop (when you're working with a guided math group) can be challenging. Encourage students to write down questions that they have for you on a sticky note and *park* them in a "parking lot"—a designated place. Students will be happy that you respect their questions, and usually they will be happy to just get their questions "off their chest."

Refer back to this lesson if you have a group of students who consistently turn to you as the teacher or immediately ask questions before giving themselves ample time to struggle at a learning station.

Materials

- sticky notes
- math problem (see sample problems at the end of this lesson)

Directions

There may be times during math workshop that you are in need of help or have a question about how to proceed. I welcome questions, and I believe that students in our class learn from one another's questions. However, I also believe that you have most of the

(continued)

answers within yourself. In a situation that you do not, one of your classmates may have the answer. What we want to avoid is asking for help before we give it our best shot. A couple of days ago we talked about best effort. What did we discuss then?

Revisit Minilesson 11 with everyone.

There are times that you may be frustrated because I am not helping you or not answering your questions. Be prepared for this, because I'm doing it to help you learn to problem solve. I do care about your learning and your thinking. I'm not ignoring you or your question.

Today, I'm going to give you a problem to try to figure out how to solve yourself. As you work on it, please use sticky notes to write down questions you may have. Please "park" your sticky notes on the corner of your desk for now. In the end, check your questions to see if you have found the answers on your own. For those questions that you have not been able to answer, turn to a classmate. As I have said, I believe in you and your ability to find most, if not all, of the answers to these questions.

As students work independently on the problem, walk around the room and look at what kind of questions they are writing down. Select questions that are strong examples of good questions. Examples from the grade 5 problem (see Sample Problems below) may be:

- Is it ok if the miles aren't exactly the same on each day?
- What do I do if the amounts aren't exactly equal?
- Should I represent the amount as a fraction or a decimal?

Reconvene as a whole class and share the examples.

SAMPLE PROBLEMS

Grade 1

- Suri has 7 baseball cards. She needs 12 baseball cards to fill a page in her collection book. How many baseball cards does Suri need to be able to fill the page?

Grade 3

- Tangier Elementary School has 432 students. Robinson Elementary has 79 more students than Tangier. How many total students are in the two schools?

Grade 5

- Rachel's aunt and uncle live 1,457 miles away. Rachel and her family plan to drive to visit, but they want to split up the drive equally in 2 days. How many miles will her family drive each day?

Exploring Math in Many Ways

Overview

In this lesson students think about the importance of exploring math in more than one way.

Many of us were taught that in a math problem, there is one—and only one—answer. And often we were taught to believe that there is only one way to solve the problem as well—the teacher's way.

The beauty of math is that, with problems that have just one correct answer, there can be many ways to arrive at that answer. And with open-ended problems, there can be many correct answers! As teachers we should respect different strategies; students who continually find alternate ways to solve problems are rewarded with a greater knowledge of number sense and problem solving. As teachers we should also challenge students to find all the answers—not just one.

It is critical to do this lesson within the first twenty days of starting math workshop. However, it is even more important to remember to include tasks like this in the days that follow.

> **The existence of several acceptable answers stimulates higher-level thinking and problem solving.**
>
> —Peter Sullivan and Pat Lilburn, authors of *Good Questions for Math Teaching, Grades K–6* (2002)

Materials

- sticky notes
- an open-ended problem (an age-appropriate task that has multiple entry points; see suggestions at the end of this lesson)

Directions

Math is such an interesting subject. Many people like it because they like to find a "right" answer. However, many don't realize that there are often several "right" answers or methods.

Think about the following problem: _____ *= 9 (As the teacher you may adjust this to fit students' needs). Now write down one way to get the answer "9."*

(continued)

Once every student is ready, ask students to share their responses with their group. Then ask every group to share two ways out loud to the whole class. Record the equations where everyone can see them.

Equations for the problem, _____ = 9, may include:

- $8 + 1 = 9$
- $9 \times 1 = 9$
- $5 + 4 = 9$
- $100 - 91 = 9$

I am now going to challenge you to work with your group to come up with as many correct ways as is possible. You can use addition, subtraction, multiplication, division, or a combination of these operations (mention only age-appropriate operations). You can also use more than two numbers.

Again, have students share their group's ideas and write the equations where everyone can see them. Have students talk about how each one is correct. Reflect on the fact that there is more than one correct "answer."

So, each group was correct. Can you imagine if we had stopped at 8 + 1 = 9? If we had stopped there, so much thinking would not have happened. So much learning and so many great ideas would not have been shared!

I appreciate that we've been respectful of one another's ideas. Even if someone used a different method or had a different idea than you, this does not mean that they are wrong. And, even if their way does not work out, we can still learn from that, as well. You have shared with me some ideas that I had not thought of for this problem!

SUGGESTED OPEN-ENDED PROBLEMS

Here are a few ideas for open-ended problems to use with this lesson and others. One of my favorite resources for these kinds of problems is the Good Questions series by authors Peter Sullivan, Pat Lilburn, Lainie Schuster, and Nancy Canavan Anderson.

- Rachel's piggy bank has 11 coins. How much money might be in Rachel's piggy bank?
- Sean has 60 cents in his piggy bank. What coin combinations might be in Sean's piggy bank?

- Francine is putting a fence around her flower garden. She has 36 feet of fencing for her garden. What might be the dimensions of her garden?

- Candace has a box of chocolates that holds 24 pieces. How might the chocolates be arranged in the box?

- The area of Harry's herb garden is 20 square feet. What might be the perimeter of the garden?

- What are some ways to make 10?

- Rhonda bought a ring for $35. What might be the combinations of bills that Rhonda could have used to pay for the ring?

- Ariel is baking cookies. She used more than $\frac{1}{4}$ cup sugar but less than $\frac{1}{3}$ cup sugar. How much sugar might Ariel have used in her cookies?

- Wally, Zola, and Yasmine together have 56 toy cars. Wally has more cars than Zola. Zola has 5 fewer cars than Yasmine. How many toy cars might each child have?

Anchor Chart

Add to your *Guidelines for Math Workshop* anchor chart:

I will explore math in more ways than one.

Checking Your Work

Overview

In this lesson students practice ways to check their work.

In math, tasking students with checking their work is more than just having them confirm right answers. Encourage students to ask themselves the following questions as part of their best practices:

✓ Am I sure about the answer?

✓ How do I know?

✓ Can I prove it another way?

✓ Can I remember a problem that was similar?

✓ Can I explain the answer in words?

✓ Does the answer jive with my estimate?

> **It's important for students to develop the mathematical practice of checking their answers to problems using different methods to decide if their answers make sense.**
>
> —Marilyn Burns, author of
> *About Teaching Mathematics,*
> *Fourth Edition* (2015)

Back in the day when I was told to check my work, I would return to my desk with my paper and skim through it to make sure that I hadn't skipped any problems. I never actually *checked* the work that I had done. This is not something that students come to school understanding. Students should look to see that their answer is reasonable. They should rework a problem to ensure the accuracy of the computation, and/or solve the problem in another way to see if the answer is the same. Just as we model for students how to work through the writing process, we need to help students explore the "checking" process.

This lesson is meant for older students (grade 3 and up). Younger students can still work on the skills of estimation and flexibility within the base ten number system.

Materials

• checklist, *Checking Your Work* (see "Directions" section)

• math problem (see sample problems at the end of this lesson)

Directions

You are probably used to hearing teachers ask you, "Have you checked your work?" or "Check it again before you turn it in." Typically this involves you returning to your seat and making sure that you didn't leave any blank answers. But there are other effective ways to check your work. Consider the following three ways to check your work:

- *Use estimation to see if your answers make sense.*

- *Ask yourself if there is another way to solve this problem.*

- *Rework the problem to see if your math is correct.*

Write the three actions on a poster and place it where everyone can see it. Title it *Checking Your Work*.

It is important to make notes about your learning and your work as you go. In a previous lesson we thought about how writing helps us clarify our thoughts. Writing down your thoughts will help you when you go back to check your work. Your numbers may not make sense to you when you return to a problem. However, if you jot down a note to yourself, you may better remember your thought process.

I'm going to ask you to solve a problem or two. After you do so, I am going to pair you up with a partner. The two of you will go through the three ways of checking your work together.

After students have completed their problem and worked together to check their work, bring them back together for a whole-class discussion. Ask them to share how checking their work was beneficial. *Did anyone find an error in their work when they checked it?*

SAMPLE PROBLEMS

- What is the greatest three-digit number whose digits total 15? Justify your answer.

- Use the digits 0, 1, 2, 3, 4, 5, 6, 7 to find the smallest answer possible in this problem:

Using Math Vocabulary

Overview

This lesson provides ideas for how students can process new vocabulary; it is most appropriate for students grade 3 and older.

In mathematics, there are many vocabulary words to learn, understand, and apply. As a part of math, take time to introduce vocabulary that may not be familiar to students. Share ways for students to process new vocabulary and make sense of it. One way may be a student-made *Math Word Wall* displayed in the classroom. For each new math word, students place the word and a picture of the word on this wall.

> Once teachers have identified what academic language students will need to know and understand in a particular math lesson, they can then plan strategies for supporting students' ability to use the language.
>
> —Rusty Bresser, Kathy Melanese, and Christine Sphar, authors of *Supporting English Language Learners in Math Class, Grades 3–5* (2009)

While all students may struggle with new vocabulary introduced in mathematics, it is imperative to consider English language learners when introducing mathematics vocabulary. Coggins and colleagues, in *English Language Learners in the Mathematics Classroom* (2009), explain that conversational language, Basic Interpersonal Communication Skills (BICS), is not as cognitively demanding and is usually acquired in one or two years. However, Cognitive Academic Language Skills (CALPS) involve thinking and communicating language uniquely found in school. CALPS can take between five and ten years to develop. This illustrates how important it is to spend time introducing mathematical academic language, especially when introducing cognitively demanding new concepts.

Materials

- *Math Word Wall* (see "Directions" section)
- Frayer Model (see illustration in "Directions" section)

Directions

We learn new words all of the time. This will be no different in math workshop; you will learn a lot of new math words. As you learn the meaning of new words, I encourage you to think about ways that will help you understand, use, and remember these words.

Consider using these words when you write about your mathematical thinking. Using your new words in writing will help you make sense of them. In a previous lesson we talked about using drawings to support our thinking. Drawing a picture of a word is an excellent way to help you understand it. We also discussed making connections to real life or to another problem. As we discuss math words, make a connection to other words that you know, even if it has nothing to do with math. Also make connections to something you have read or done in previous math lessons.

Now I'm going to introduce you to a word that may or may not be new to you. It is a word that we will be using in future lessons.

Introduce a math word that could cause some confusion. This may be a new math word for many students. Encourage students to talk about this word with a partner. Then introduce students to the following Frayer Model, which is shown using the word *hour*. A Frayer Model is a graphic organizer that helps to make meaning of a word or concept by considering examples and non-examples, as well as definitions and facts. Ask students to create and fill in a Frayer Model using a selected word.

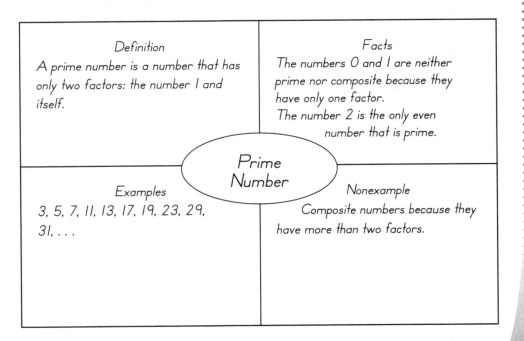

To conclude, have a student add the word (including a picture of it) to the *Math Word Wall.*

Anchor Chart

Add to your *Guidelines for Math Workshop* anchor chart:

I will use ways to help me understand and remember new vocabulary.

Reflecting and Sharing

Overview

In this lesson students reflect on their learning and think about the value of reflection.

Reflecting on what we've learned is key in everything we do. Reflection can be done formally or informally and in a variety of ways. As teachers we can help students with reflection by practicing the following guidelines:

> There are two cognitive processes that are key in students' efforts to understand mathematics—reflection and communication.
>
> —James Hiebert, Thomas P. Carpenter, Elizabeth Fennema, Karen C. Fuson, Diana Wearne, Hanlie Murray, Alwyn Oliver, and Piet Human, authors of *Making Sense: Teaching and Learning Mathematics with Understanding* (1997)

- Provide enough wait time for students to reflect.
- Provide a supportive environment in which everyone is comfortable with risk taking and sharing.
- Prompt reviews of the learning situation by asking what is known, what is not yet known, and what has been learned.
- Provide authentic tasks, open-ended tasks, and inquiry-based activities to encourage reflective thinking.
- Prompt reflection by asking for reasons, proof, and evidence.
- Provide students with vocabulary tools for reflection when needed.
- Provide collaborative learning environments and small-group activities to allow students to see others' points of view.
- Promote reflective journal writing; students should record thoughts and reasons that support what they think while keeping an awareness of others' ideas.

As teachers, we often feel that time is not available for reflection. However, this a critical time for students to learn about the thinking of others, compare this thinking to their own, and make important connections.

Remember, even very young mathematicians have brilliant ideas to share; don't be tempted to skip the reflection just because your students are young.

Materials

- open-ended problem
- math journal, one per student (if you do not use math journals, a notebook or paper will work)

Directions

Give students an open-ended problem (an age-appropriate task that has multiple entry points).

Let's take a look at this task. Take some time to work on this task independently. Remember what we agreed to a few days ago when we talked about working independently. Will someone remind us of some of the things we discussed?

Before this lesson, it is important, as the teacher, to do the math and anticipate possible student strategies. As students are working, walk around and look for these strategies. If students are "stuck," remember to ask questions rather than give answers.

Revisit Minilesson 13 for possible questions to consider asking when a student is "stuck."

Ask students to share their strategies and/or solutions. However, refrain from merely asking who wants to share. Instead, sequence those who share based on the strategies you saw them using. This will help the students make important connections to the mathematics and to the strategies. Following the task, prompt further reflection by asking a question such as:

- What was your task or outcome for this activity?
- What are some important concepts or ideas that you discovered?
- How did you solve the problem or complete your task? Explain.
- Would you make revisions to your work if you had to do it again? Explain.
- How could the mathematics in this problem be important to a real-life situation?
- What was easy for you? Most difficult for you? Why?

Allow students time to write and/or discuss their reflections for the lesson. Using their math journals, they may record strategies that they saw or write in words about their discoveries. Encourage this daily.

The following are examples of students' journal reflections. For other ideas for reflection options, see Chapter 9.

(continued)

EXAMPLES OF STUDENT REFLECTIONS

Kindergarten

When asked to write about which learning station was her favorite, Julianna wrote, *I love the dot game the most today.*

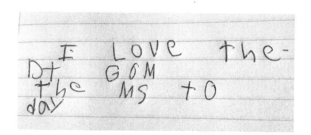

Grade 2

When asked about a strategy that he found interesting today, Ronan wrote, *My teacher gave me this problem 47 + 35. Gianna had a cool way. She started with 47. I might try her way tomorrow.*

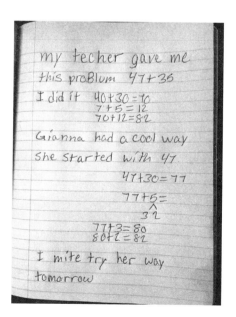

Anchor Chart

Add to your *Guidelines for Math Workshop* anchor chart:

I will reflect on my learning.

Understanding the Guidelines for Math Workshop

Overview

This lesson is a culmination and review of the eighteen previous minilessons.

At this point, upon completing the previous eighteen minilessons, your classroom should have a *Guidelines for Math Workshop* chart displayed. Treat this chart as a living document—one that can be continually revisited. As students engage in math workshop, they may want to clarify and/or add to some of the statements on the chart.

> Math workshop can be designed to support authentic mathematical investigations while providing opportunities for skill development and expectations for work of high quality.
>
> —Linda Dacey, Jayne Bamford Lynch, and Rebeka Eston Salemi, authors of *How to Differentiate Your Math Instruction* (2013)

Materials

- *Guidelines for Math Workshop* chart

Directions

Everything that we have been talking about will lead us to having successful math workshop. I believe in each of you and your ability to be successful in math.

Math workshop describes how our math class will run this year. It is very similar to reading and writing workshop. However, it may be different from what you are used to when learning math. Therefore, it is important for us to understand the expectations for each day.

Many of the expectations we have already talked about, and some we will be describing and discussing in more detail soon. Let's review and summarize what we have recorded on our chart, Guidelines for Math Workshop.

Give students time to discuss with each other and share with the whole class what they understand about each of the guidelines listed on the chart. You may choose to have students give an example and a nonexample, or act each statement out.

If you've completed the minilessons in this chapter, the statements on your chart will likely read as follows:

- I will be an active listener.

(continued)

- I will make connections between math and the world around me.
- I will talk about my thinking in math.
- I will write about my thinking in math.
- I will use different strategies to help me solve problems.
- I will do my best work whether working collaboratively or independently.
- I will use math tools and manipulatives responsibly to help my thinking.
- I will represent my thinking visually when helpful.
- I will give my best effort and be respectful to my classmates.
- I will transition from one activity to the next quickly and without disrupting others.
- I will help others get started and get unstuck as needed.
- I will persevere through difficult math, never give up, and believe in myself.
- I will explore math in more ways than one.
- I will check my work.
- I will use ways to help me understand and remember new vocabulary.
- I will reflect on my learning.

Any time that you find that students are struggling with these guidelines, return to the chart and corresponding minilesson.

 VIDEO CLIP 2.5

Understanding the Guidelines for Math Workshop

In this clip Ms. Lempp revisits, with a class of second graders, some of the expectations for math workshop. As you watch this clip, consider the following questions:

- What is the importance of having the rules for math workshop come from the students?

- What are some of the math workshop expectations you find most challenging in your classroom and why?

To view this video clip, scan the QR code or access via mathsolutions.com/mathworkshop25

Putting It All Together

Overview

As previously mentioned, the lessons in this chapter are not meant to replace math instruction for twenty days. These lessons, when combined with your curriculum, will allow you to cover important math material while establishing the routines and procedures needed for math workshop.

> In math workshop, I'm so good at math and I have so much fun.
>
> —third grader, after four months of math workshop

The lesson that follows provides an example of how to use one of the previous nineteen minilessons alongside your day's math lesson. You may use this as a template for carrying out all of the minilessons.

If you haven't already, start math workshop—maybe not with all the components, but with a few (remember, Go Slow to Go Fast!). Each following day you will build on this day, adding more choice, independence, and time for guided groups. Don't worry—it will be great! And if it isn't, reflect on and identify what went wrong. Refer back to the lessons here to help fine-tune the process.

Math Skill: Grade 3, Multiplying whole numbers up to the twelves tables	
Minilesson 12: Transitioning Between Activities	
Materials: Unifix cube arrays, multiplication cards, timer or timer tool, counters, centimeter cubes, graph paper	
Introduction	*We are creating a mathematics classroom that ensures that each of you have the best opportunity to learn. It is important that we always challenge ourselves and also respect the learning of others. In order for our system to work best for math workshop and for us to get the most out of our math time, it is important that everyone spend as little time transitioning from one activity to another. Transitions should be smooth and quick.*

(continued)

	This means that when you stop one activity, you clean up your materials and return them the way you found them. You quickly gather any materials needed for your next activity and get started immediately. Wasted time adds up, and over the course of a year, a lot of math learning time can be lost because of transitions.
Exploration Learning stations (simulation)	*Let's practice transitioning from one activity to another. Each group has a collection of Unifix cubes at their table. These cubes will be used to create arrays. Choose one of the multiplication cards provided, and create an array with the cubes that matches the problem on the card. Work on this activity for about 10 minutes. When I give you the signal, clean up the materials, return them, and gather your materials for the next activity.* Use a timer or timer tool to help students understand how long it takes them to transition from one activity to another. Materials for the next activity should be placed in a consistent location. Follow the steps again, only with this activity: Students complete a matching activity where they match a multiplication problem to an answer or picture. This lesson can be repeated as many times as necessary until the desired results are achieved.
Reflection	*On average, it took our class about __ minutes to transition from one activity to the next. While speed is important, I also want you to remember that it is equally important to be safe and respectful of materials and of each other. We need to walk, not run, when we move from station to station, and we need to make sure that no materials are left behind.* *While all transitions are not going to be timed in this manner and many of our transitions will be happening at different times when we fully implement math workshop, I hope that this lesson allows you to realize the expectations that we have when it comes to transitions in the classroom.* *Please discuss with your partner at least one way that we can all help to decrease the transition time while still being safe.* Ask for a few students to share ideas that they discussed with their partner.

Connecting the Chapter to Your Practice

- Which of the three buckets (see page 33) do you believe are currently the "fullest" in your classroom? Which do you want to work on? How?

- Consider ways that you build community with the students in your classroom. What has been successful?

- Consider your expectations for routines and procedures in your math class. How are students encouraged to work together? How do they have access to tools and manipulatives? How do they have choice in the activities they complete?

- What do you want to be mindful of as you shift toward math workshop? What changes might you want to make to set yourself up for success?

Decide Your Math Workshop Structure

STEP 3

In math class, sometimes the focus is on students learning new content. Other times students need more time to practice the content and the skills. Yet other times they need opportunities to explore complex mathematical ideas and relationships. Math workshop meets these needs by allowing you as the teacher to choose how you want to structure your mathematics instructional time—**the teacher intentionally chooses the math workshop structure that will best support the lesson.**

As I figured out math workshop, I found that my class started to take on the look of one of three structures: *Task and Share*; *Focus Lesson, Guided Math, and Learning Stations*; and *Guided Math and Learning Stations*. These structures are introduced at a glance in columns 2–4 of Table A on the next page; compare them to a traditional classroom structure, listed in the first column.

One thing is for sure—the three math workshop structures differ a great deal from the traditional model of mathematics instruction. The traditional model, which many of us are likely most familiar with from our childhood days in school, still happens in classrooms today. Let's take a closer look at it compared to the math workshop structures.

The traditional classroom structure opens with a warm-up that tends to be a worksheet. Unfortunately, the warm-up often lacks engagement and is not accessible to all students.

TRADITIONAL CLASSROOM		MATH WORKSHOP: TASK AND SHARE		MATH WORKSHOP: FOCUS LESSON, GUIDED MATH, AND LEARNING STATIONS			MATH WORKSHOP: GUIDED MATH AND LEARNING STATIONS		
5 minutes	WARM-UP	5–10 minutes	NUMBER SENSE ROUTINE	5–10 minutes	NUMBER SENSE ROUTINE		5–10 minutes	NUMBER SENSE ROUTINE	
10 minutes	HOMEWORK CHECK	30 minutes	MATH TASK	15 minutes	FOCUS LESSON		45 minutes	GUIDED MATH	LEARNING STATIONS
30 minutes	TEACHER MODELED PRACTICE			30 minutes	GUIDED MATH	LEARNING STATIONS			
10 minutes	INDEPENDENT PRACTICE	20–25 minutes	TASK SHARE WITH STUDENT REFLECTION	5–10 minutes	STUDENT REFLECTION		5–10 minutes	STUDENT REFLECTION	
5 minutes	HOMEWORK ASSIGNMENT								

Table A. Comparing a traditional classroom structure to the three math workshop structures

For a one-page summary of the three math workshop structures, see Reproducible 14.

Often some students finish in one minute, while others do not even get started. This is followed by at least fifteen minutes of checking homework. Some students know they have the right answers because their parents reviewed their work the night before. Others are avoiding the discussion because they did not do their homework, and several more have their heads buried in their desks or backpacks, insisting they did it, but just can't find it. At this point, one-third of the math class is over, and the teacher may have only reached about one-third of the students. Then everyone moves into thirty minutes of teacher modeled/guided practice, which really turns out to be the teacher at the front of the class, talking *at* the students and showing the students how to do the problem step-by-step. There is little student discussion, exploration, or sense making. This continues until the teacher feels that the majority of students can replicate the steps when given a problem independently to complete. Finally, with fifteen minutes of class left, it's time for students to independently solve problems in the same way the teacher solved them. The teacher walks around the room and monitors students as

How does a traditional classroom structure differ from any of the three math workshop structures proposed in Table A (on page 100)? Which structure resonates with your instructional time? Which structure are you most curious about trying?

they work on the assigned problem, and then is startled to find, in looking up at the clock, that math time is almost over. There is no time to reflect on the learning, so the teacher points to the assignment that is written on the board for homework. This cycle continues the next day, and the next, and the next.

It is my hope that you will find the three math workshop structures, introduced in depth in the next three chapters, to undoubtedly be your preferred model of instruction. In this section, considered step 3 of the 5 steps to a successful math workshop, you'll have the opportunity to:

- learn the benefits of each of the three structures,
- understand when the structure would be most supportive of learning,
- learn best practices in implementing each structure,
- see samples of each structure,
- gain an understanding of what each structure looks like in a math block, and
- envision what each structure might look like in your own classroom.

> See Figure 10–1 in Chapter 10 for a framework to help you decide your math workshop structure.

Chapters in Step 3

Task and Share Structure

CHAPTER 3

 **VIDEO CLIP 3.1** ·

The Task and Share Structure in Action

This clip highlights excerpts from Ms. McGonigal's third-grade class as she facilitates a Task and Share math workshop structure. The math task is solving the story problem: *Mr. Gawan is 73 inches. Ms. Reynolds is 61 inches. How much taller is Mr. Gawan than Ms. Reynolds?* As you watch the clip, consider these questions:

- What math workshop characteristics do you see happening in this video (see Chapter 1, page 4, Seven Math Workshop Characteristics)?
- What do you notice about the task the teacher selected to have the students do?
- What surprises you about this way of doing math workshop?
- How is what is happening in this classroom different or similar to what is happening in your classroom?
- What questions might you have after watching this clip?

To view this video clip, scan the QR code or access via mathsolutions.com/mathworkshop31

· ·

What Is *Task and Share*?

MATH WORKSHOP: TASK AND SHARE		MATH WORKSHOP: FOCUS LESSON, GUIDED MATH, AND LEARNING STATIONS			MATH WORKSHOP: GUIDED MATH AND LEARNING STATIONS		
5 minutes	NUMBER SENSE ROUTINE An engaging, accessible, purposeful routine to begin your math class that promotes a community of positive mathematics discussion and thinking.	5–10 minutes	NUMBER SENSE ROUTINE		5–10 minutes	NUMBER SENSE ROUTINE	
30 minutes	MATH TASK A problem-solving task that students work on in small groups. The teacher circulates and probes student thinking through questions. The task typically has multiple entry points, allowing for all students to have access to the problem.	15 minutes	FOCUS LESSON		45 minutes	GUIDED MATH	LEARNING STATIONS
		30 minutes	GUIDED MATH	LEARNING STATIONS			
20–25 minutes	TASK SHARE WITH STUDENT REFLECTION A math share in which students come together as a whole class and discuss the various strategies they used to solve the problem. Students ask questions, clarify their thinking, modify their work, and add to their collection of strategies.	5–10 minutes	STUDENT REFLECTION		5–10 minutes	STUDENT REFLECTION	

The Task and Share structure opens with a number sense routine, just like the other two math workshop structures begin. This routine engages all learners, promoting discourse, respect, and risk taking (see Chapter 6 for more on number sense routines). Then, instead of a focus lesson or learning stations, students engage in a math task. The teacher purposely selects the problem-solving task; typically it is a word problem. In presenting it, the teacher is careful not to give too much away, allowing the students to really grapple with the task and make sense of what is being asked. This structure is very different from a traditional one. The teacher is not modeling how to solve the problem, and the teacher refrains from identifying strategies or operations to use. Rather, the teacher's role is one of facilitator. While students work on the task, the teacher monitors their work and asks questions to help support students who are stuck or to help students who need clarification. The last twenty-five minutes are reserved for task share with student reflection, in which the teacher invites students to share their work in a systematic way while supporting connections among their strategies (see Chapter 9 for more on reflections).

Why Use Task and Share?

This structure promotes the discovery of *why*, the rationale, behind a math skill students are learning. The structure requires us as teachers to move from the traditional way of thinking—that students must master the skill in a naked number problem *before* students use the skill in a complex word problem. Rather, it gives students the opportunity to dive right into a problem-solving task, explore it, and constructively struggle. We now know that we should not wait for a skill to be developed before engaging students in rich problem solving. When mathematical concepts are introduced in context, students have a better understanding of why they are performing computation on numbers and why this would be something that would be valuable as a lifelong skill.

What Is a Naked Number Problem?

Many of us were taught mathematics in much the same way. We were shown a problem and told a set of steps to follow in order to solve the problem. Those steps, when followed correctly, produced the one right answer. I refer to this as a "naked number problem." In this resource naked number problems are defined as problems that are *not* presented in context through a word or story problem. (See Figure 3–1 on the next page.)

NAKED NUMBER PROBLEM	PROBLEM-SOLVING TASK: WORD PROBLEM
The teacher writes the following on the board and asks students to independently solve it: 216 − 37	The teacher tasks students with solving the following word problem, often in partners or small groups: *The trip from our house to grandma's house is 216 miles. We have driven 37 miles so far. How many miles do we have yet to drive?*

Figure 3–1. Naked number problem versus a word problem

A naked number problem often invites the traditional algorithm—a set of prescribed steps or procedures. Presented in the way shown in Figure 3–1, this problem rarely invites student-invented strategies, thus limiting the number of strategies that students will consider and share. It does not encourage mathematical reasoning. This is not to say that naked number problems don't have a place in the mathematics classroom. Using naked number problems for *number talks* (see Chapter 6) encourages mental math strategies and conversations.

One might question why an entire math class would be spent on just one problem-solving task. We all can understand the pressure to try to do more, especially when we feel that we are behind in our pacing. However, using this structure a couple of times each unit is well worth it. You will learn so much about your students, and your students will learn much from their peers.

When Should I Use Task and Share?

The Task and Share structure is especially powerful when introducing a new unit, though it can also be used numerous times in a unit. Let's consider two scenarios based on the problems.

First, envision a class in which, as part of planning for an upcoming unit on multiplying fractions, a teacher presents the naked number problem (see Figure 3–2) to students. As teachers we may choose to do this because we feel that giving students a problem-solving task instead will make it more difficult for students to understand the mathematics. However, when performing operations with fractions, many students encounter misconceptions because they try to apply their whole-number understandings to fractions. Students know that when they multiply two whole numbers, the product is larger than the factors. So, when they see a problem like $7 \times \frac{1}{4} = $ ___, they anticipate that the answer is going to be larger than 7.

NAKED NUMBER PROBLEM	PROBLEM-SOLVING TASK: WORD PROBLEM
$7 \times \frac{1}{4} = \underline{\hspace{1cm}}$	Sue ran $\frac{1}{4}$ of a mile each day for 7 days. How far did Sue run in those 7 days?

Figure 3–2. Two ways to present a problem

Let's now envision a class where the teacher chooses to introduce the unit by showing students the word problem (see Figure 3–2). This is a problem that students, even without prior knowledge of multiplying fractions, can solve. There are different entry points for students to be successful with this problem. The teacher realizes that students have exposure to adding and subtracting fractions and hence knows students could draw a picture or use addition. They might choose to make a connection to repeated addition with whole numbers as multiplication. Students can then write a number sentence that would represent this problem and what they did. However students may choose to solve the problem, doing so will help them understand *why* they would want to multiply fractions. It will also help them understand why the answer is going to be smaller than seven and why we don't apply the same rules for whole numbers to fractions.

Reflect on It!

Revisit Figure 3–2. How might the context provided for the word problem support student understanding? What does this provide for students that the naked number problem does not?

One of the most exciting parts about a Task and Share is that as teachers we will hear the most remarkable ideas coming from students—as long as we refrain from telling them they have to do things a certain way. When students feel there are more ways than one to solve a problem, and multiple ways are acceptable, you will start seeing many strategies surface. For the word problem shown in Figure 3–2, students in my classroom came up with the following strategies. (See Figure 3–3 on the next page.)

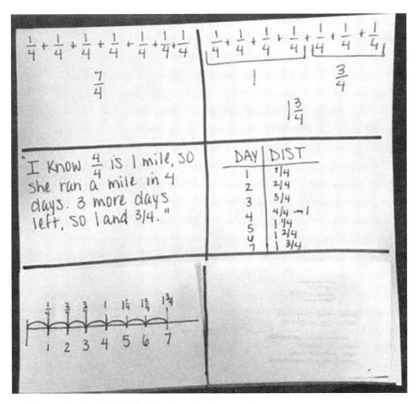

Figure 3–3. Student strategies for solving the word problem in Figure 3–2

The Traditional Algorithm

It is imperative that students have the opportunity to explore student-invented strategies prior to being exposed to the traditional algorithm. This exploration will help them compute flexibly, accurately, and efficiently. It will also help them understand *why* the algorithm works while providing them with strategies that they can choose from depending on the numbers they are working with.

Think about the naked number problem $200 - 2 =$ _____. Do we want students to rely on the traditional algorithm in this situation? Of course not! In fact, many students will make errors when working with problems like this if they have only been taught the traditional algorithm because they have a fragile understanding of regrouping. Figure 3–4 on the next page shares some errors that students have made with this problem.

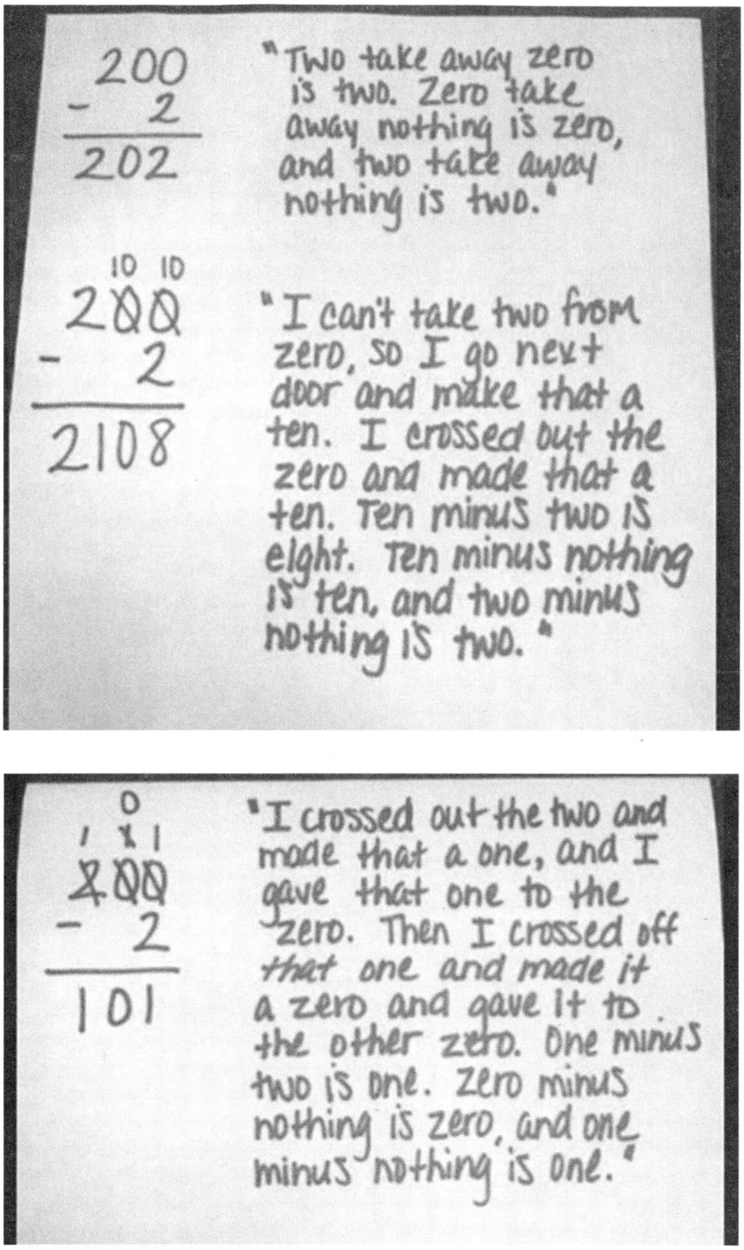

$$\begin{array}{r} 200 \\ -2 \\ \hline 202 \end{array}$$

"Two take away zero is two. Zero take away nothing is zero, and two take away nothing is two."

$$\begin{array}{r} \overset{1010}{2\cancel{0}\cancel{0}} \\ -2 \\ \hline 2108 \end{array}$$

"I can't take two from zero, so I go next door and make that a ten. I crossed out the zero and made that a ten. Ten minus two is eight. Ten minus nothing is ten, and two minus nothing is two."

$$\begin{array}{r} \overset{\overset{0}{\cancel{1}}1}{\overset{1}{\cancel{2}}\cancel{0}\cancel{0}} \\ -2 \\ \hline 101 \end{array}$$

"I crossed out the two and made that a one, and I gave that one to the zero. Then I crossed off that one and made it a zero and gave it to the other zero. One minus two is one. Zero minus nothing is zero, and one minus nothing is one."

Figure 3–4. Examples of student explanations for solving *200 – 2* using the traditional algorithm

What Should I Keep in Mind When Selecting a Task?

When making decisions about which task to use with your students, keep the following characteristics of rich tasks in mind:

- Rich tasks have a context.
- Rich tasks have multiple entry points for solving them.
- Rich tasks allow for different ways to solve them.
- Rich tasks require mathematical reasoning.

In order to determine if a task meets these criteria, as teachers we should first solve the problem ourselves and attempt to find as many ways to solve it as possible. Let's try this with the following task:

Grandma's House

The trip from our house to Grandma's house is 216 miles. We have driven 37 miles so far. How many miles do we have yet to drive?

What are some of the strategies you think your students will come up with to solve this problem? Jot down your ideas before referencing a few possible strategies in Figure 3–5.

STRATEGY	RECORDING
Compensation	216 − 37 216 − 40 = 176 *Taking 40 away is easier than 37.* 176 + 3 = 179 *I added three since I took three too many away.*
Adding Up Using Open Number Line	*The answer is in my jumps.* + 3 + 60 + 100 + 16 = 179 37 40 100 200 216
Transforming Numbers	216 ⟶ change to 199 + 17 − 37 − 37 162 + 17 = 179 *That was a lot easier since there was no regrouping.*

Figure 3–5. Student strategies to solve *Grandma's House* task

When selecting problem-solving tasks, it is also important to expose students to different problem types, as referenced in the resource, *Children's Mathematics: Cognitively Guided Instruction* by Thomas Carpenter and colleagues (Carpenter et al. 1999). Many problem-solving tasks that we use tend to be "result unknown" problems. In order to promote reasoning and problem solving, students should see other problem types. (See Figure 3–6.) After all, we don't want all subtraction problems to be seen as take away. By exposing students to other problem types, they will come to think about computation in variety of ways.

Join Problems	**Result Unknown** Rachel had 7 stickers. Manuel gave her 5 more. How many stickers does Rachel have altogether?	**Change Unknown** Rachel had 7 stickers. Manuel gave her some more. Now Rachel has 12 stickers. How many stickers did Manuel give Rachel?	**Initial Unknown** Rachel had some stickers. Manuel gave her 5 more. Now Rachel has 12 stickers. How many stickers did Rachel have to begin with?
Separate Problems	**Result Unknown** Rachel had 12 stickers. She gave 5 stickers to Manuel. How many stickers does Rachel have now?	**Change Unknown** Rachel had 12 stickers. She gave some to Manuel. Now she has 7 stickers. How many did she give to Manuel?	**Initial Unknown** Rachel had some stickers. She gave 5 to Manuel. Now Rachel has 7 stickers left. How many stickers did Rachel have to begin with?
Part–Part–Whole	**Whole Unknown** Rachel has 7 flower stickers and 5 heart stickers. How many stickers does Rachel have altogether?	**Part Unknown** Rachel has 12 stickers. Five of them are heart stickers and the rest are flower stickers. How many flower stickers does Rachel have?	
Compare	**Difference Unknown** Rachel has 12 stickers and Manuel has 7 stickers. How many more stickers does Rachel have than Manuel?	**Larger Unknown** Manuel has 7 stickers. Rachel has 5 more stickers than Manuel. How many stickers does Rachel have?	**Smaller Unknown** Rachel has 12 stickers. She has 7 more stickers than Manuel. How many stickers does Manuel have?
Grouping	**Multiplication** Rachel has 4 pages of stickers. There are 6 stickers on each page. How many stickers does Rachel have?	**Measurement Division** Rachel has 24 stickers. They are organized with 6 stickers on each page. How many pages of stickers does Rachel have?	**Partitive Division** Rachel has 4 pages of stickers with the same number of stickers on each page. She has 24 stickers in all. How many stickers are on each page?

Figure 3–6. Various problem types students should be exposed to

What Does Task and Share Look Like in a Lesson?

In order to ensure that your class time is used efficiently for the Task and Share structure, considering following Smith and Stein's *5 Practices for Orchestrating Effective Mathematics Discussions* (2011), summarized here:

1. *Anticipate.* As the teacher, it is important that when you choose a task, you do the math yourself. It is even better if you do the task with your colleagues. Often, after doing a task, I realize that the task isn't really appropriate, or I realize it needs to be adapted in some way to fit the students or standards. It is also important that when you choose a task, you do so with purpose, carefully selecting the numbers used. Every move you make with the task should be purposeful, and you should anticipate answers, strategies, misconceptions, common errors, and vocabulary that may be challenging.

2. *Monitor.* As students are working on the problem independently and collaboratively, circulate, facilitating student thinking by asking probing questions. If you see a student who is stuck, ask questions rather than giving a first step or telling the way that you would solve the problem. Look for evidence of the strategies that you anticipated, and remain open to the idea that a student may have a strategy that you did not anticipate.

3. *Select.* When you see an example of a strategy you anticipated, "select" it by asking the student if they are willing to share their strategy with the whole group. Asking permission is also a way to make the student feel comfortable with whole-group sharing.

4. *Sequence.* Determine the order in which to share the strategies you've selected. Consider ordering them from the most concrete to the most abstract to help students make connections.

5. *Connect.* As students are sharing their work, use talk moves (see Minilesson 3 in Chapter 2) to keep all students engaged in the conversation and ask questions to elicit connections between the strategies.

Let's look at the Task and Share structure broken up by component so that we can examine what it might look like and sound like in a lesson. (See Figure 3–7 on the next page.) For a lesson template to support you in creating your own Task and Share lesson plan, see Reproducible 1.

Math Workshop Lesson Plan: Task and Share

Date:	Big Idea:
Number Sense Routine:	
Task:	

Anticipated Strategies:		

Student Reflection:

Reproducible 1. Math Workshop Lesson Plan: Task and Share (blank)

See Reproducible 1 for a Math Workshop Lesson Plan template to help you plan a Task and Share.

TIME	COMPONENT	WHAT DOES IT LOOK LIKE AND SOUND LIKE?	WHY DO IT?
5 minutes	Number Sense Routine: Count Around	Students come to the carpet and sit in a circle. Tell students that they are going to count by twos around the room. Some questions to ask before starting: *If I start by saying, "zero" and we go around the circle this way, what number do you think the last student, [insert student name here] will say?* *OK, so what number do you think the person in the middle, [insert student name here], will say?* *Where do you think it might become challenging to continue counting?* *If we skip-counted by fives would our last number be more or less than counting by twos? What if we counted by ones?*	It is important to start each class period together as a whole group. This promotes a sense of community. Students should be encouraged to talk in the first five minutes of the class period, be engaged in the learning, and have a positive experience. There are many number sense routines that can be used as a way to begin math class. See Chapter 6 for more ideas. Look for something that is engaging, purposeful, and accessible to all students.
30 minutes	Math Task	Introduction/Launch Ask students if they have ever had to share something with anyone. Tell them a story: *I was having lunch last week in the teacher's lounge. I brought a sandwich. Then, [insert teacher from your school] walked in and realized that she had forgotten her lunch. I decided to share my sandwich with her so that she would not be hungry. What do you think I did?* *Turn to a shoulder partner and tell them what you think happened.* Take responses from students.	It is important to give students an opportunity to explore and understand the key vocabulary and key mathematical ideas in the problem. During this time, you will want to ask an inclusive question in order to get "buy-in" from all students. An inclusive question is one that everyone will say yes to. In this case, the inclusive question is about sharing. All students most likely have experience with sharing something.

Figure 3–7. What a Task and Share structure might look and sound like in a lesson

TIME	COMPONENT	WHAT DOES IT LOOK LIKE AND SOUND LIKE?	WHY DO IT?
		Exploration: Independent Work *As a class, we are going to be looking at a problem today about children and brownies.* Give students a few minutes to think about this task independently. Be sure to tell students that during this time, everyone is to work quietly. The task: *Four children are on a picnic. There are 6 brownies for them to share equally. How much brownie will each child get if they eat all the brownies themselves without having any left over?*	Students process at different speeds; first giving them quiet, independent time with the task allows everyone an opportunity to think. Students are more likely to have something to share with their partner when they do begin working collaboratively if they have been given the opportunity to think first. Asking students to immediately turn and start working with a partner will often result in the strongest student taking over the work while the partner simply follows; the student who needed more time to process is left without a real job to do—they simply copy the work of their partner and move on.
		Exploration: Collaborative Work Encourage students to talk about their thinking with a partner. Ask them to refrain from telling an answer; rather they should explain what their strategy is or where they might be stuck if they have not been able to think of a strategy to use.	Traditionally, sharing answers in mathematics has been seen as cheating. It is important to encourage students to be comfortable with sharing their work. Have students look at what their partner wrote down, ask their partner questions about what they did, and explain to one another their thinking. This does not come naturally for students, therefore, it is important that they are granted this "permission."

Figure 3–7. *(Continued)*

(continued)

TIME	COMPONENT	WHAT DOES IT LOOK LIKE AND SOUND LIKE?	WHY DO IT?
		Exploration: Additional Time Tell students that they can continue to work collaboratively and record their thinking or the strategy of a peer on their paper. Tell them that they can keep working using their original strategy or even try out one of their classmates' strategies.	At this point, students should now have a strategy if they didn't have one before. Give them time to try the strategy out. If this additional time isn't provided, students may lose the chance to practice an idea that they think might work for them. Students who had a strategy from the start can use this time to try out another strategy and/or one from their partner. Emphasize that during this time, using someone else's strategy is not seen as "copying" or "cheating." Learning from one another is encouraged and is part of the mathematics community.
20–25 minutes	Task Share with Student Reflection	To encourage students to reflect on their learning, carefully select a few strategies students have used and invite those students to come up and show and share the strategies. Project the strategies where everyone can see them. As students share, ask probing questions that to help clarify the thinking for others. Use talk moves to help support students' understanding of their peers' strategies and to make connections among the strategies.	It is important to be thoughtful about the strategies you share as a whole class. Look for certain strategies, and don't just ask for students to raise their hand if they want or are willing to share. Help students make connections between strategies and understand one another's strategies by using teacher talk moves (see Minilesson 3 in Chapter 2). For more on student reflections, see Chapter 9.

Figure 3–7. *(Continued)*

Math Workshop Look–Fors Sheet

If you are an administrator observing math workshop and considering what you should be looking for, or if you are a classroom teacher and wish to reflect on your own practice and do a self-assessment, you might consider using the "Look Fors" (Reproducible 2) for the Task and Share structure.

See Reproducible 2 for "look-fors" for Task and Share.

Math Workshop Look-Fors: Task and Share

Whether you are an administrator going into classrooms and needing to know what to look for when it comes to math workshop or a teacher who is reflecting on your practice and doing self-assessment, this "Look-Fors" list will help as you consider what should be happening in this structure.

TASK AND SHARE	
5 minutes	NUMBER SENSE ROUTINE ❏ Routine is engaging. ❏ Student discourse is happening. ❏ Routine is accessible by all students.

30 minutes	MATH TASK
	Task is/has:
	  ❏ significant content
	  ❏ open-ended
	  ❏ high cognitive demand
	  ❏ multiple ways to show competence
	❏ Task is appropriately "launched" so that all students have access.
	❏ Teacher doesn't "give away" the math before students begin.
	❏ Teacher doesn't "rescue" during student work time.
	❏ Teacher monitors student work and probes student thinking with questions rather than answers.

20–25 minutes	TASK SHARE WITH STUDENT REFLECTION
	❏ Students share out about the various strategies that were used. Students ask questions, clarify their thinking, modify their work, and add to their collection of strategies in their tool box.
	Teacher:
	  ❏ anticipates, early on, student strategies
	  ❏ thoughtfully selects strategies to be shared
	  ❏ purposefully sequences the strategies to share
	  ❏ connects student strategies
	  ❏ shows no favoritism toward any one particular strategy
	  ❏ uses talk moves to engage all students in discussion about strategies

Reproducible 2. Math Workshop Look-Fors: Task and Share

How *Not* to Introduce a Task

- *Don't tell students what operation to use.* For example, avoid stating, "Today, we are going to be focusing on multiplying fractions." By doing this, as teachers we immediately limit the variety of strategies that students may come up with. Those who already know how to multiply fractions will be successful, and those who don't know how or don't remember are set up for failure. They feel stuck and don't know where to start.

- *Don't do an example problem first.* As teachers we may have a tendency to show students what to do; in this case we might model a strategy. By doing this, we give the impression that there is a right strategy and a wrong strategy; the teacher's way is the right way. Students are then more likely to solve the problem the teacher's way, even though they might not really understand it.

- *Don't look for key words that are supposed to serve as a clue to the operation.* By doing this you are telling students that there is only one operation that is acceptable for a problem. However, we know that the operations are connected. There was a time in my early teaching days in which I created anchor charts for problems. These charts would include key vocabulary and what operation to use. For example, my chart might have read:

  - If you see the words *in all*, you should add.
  - If you see the words *how many more*, you should subtract.

  However, let's take a look at a problem like this:

  I have 10 pencils, but I need 17 pencils. How many more pencils do I need to buy?
  Based on my anchor chart, students would need to set up this problem as $17 - 10 = 7$. However, couldn't they also count on from 10 to 17 to find the answer? Many children find solving using addition strategies easier than subtraction.

  By assigning an operation to a key word, as teachers we take away students' opportunities to do their own thinking around the problem—to grapple with it. We take away the connections that students are making between the operations. And we may take away their preferred approach to solving a problem.

Connecting the Chapter to Your Practice

- How does what you currently do in your classroom connect to the components of a Task and Share structure?

- What is your vision of a math workshop at this point? How does the Task and Share structure fit with that vision? In what ways does it not?

- What do you want to be mindful of when you next introduce a problem-solving task in your mathematics class?

- What are some questions you can ask students when they are stuck in order to refrain from showing *your* way of solving the problem?

- As you consider your upcoming unit, how might you use the Task and Share structure of math workshop in it?

 **VIDEO CLIP 3.1** ·

The Task and Share Structure in Action, Revisited

Rewatch this clip, now bringing the insights you've learned from this chapter into play. Consider the following questions:
- What do you notice in this video since watching it the first time and reading this chapter?

- Revisit the characteristics of rich tasks listed on page 110 of this chapter. In what ways does the task in this math workshop mirror these characteristics?

To view this video clip, scan the QR code or access via mathsolutions.com/mathworkshop31

· ·

CHAPTER 4

Focus Lesson, Guided Math, and Learning Stations Structure

The Focus Lesson, Guided Math, and Learning Stations Structure in Action

This clip highlights excerpts from Ms. Hrabak's fourth-grade class as she facilitates a Focus Lesson, Guided Math, and Learning Stations math workshop structure. As you watch this clip, consider these questions:

- What math workshop characteristics do you see happening in this clip (see Chapter 1, page 4, Seven Math Workshop Characteristics)?
- What do you notice about the focus lesson the teacher selected to have the students do?
- What do you notice about what is happening in the guided math groups? How is this similar to and different from what is happening in the learning stations?
- What surprises you about this way of doing math workshop?
- How is what is happening in this classroom different or similar to what is happening in your classroom?
- What questions might you have after watching this clip?

To view this video clip, scan the QR code or access via mathsolutions.com/mathworkshop41

What Is *Focus Lesson, Guided Math, and Learning Stations?*

MATH WORKSHOP: TASK AND SHARE		MATH WORKSHOP: FOCUS LESSON, GUIDED MATH, AND LEARNING STATIONS			MATH WORKSHOP: GUIDED MATH AND LEARNING STATIONS		
5–10 minutes	NUMBER SENSE ROUTINE	5–10 minutes	NUMBER SENSE ROUTINE An engaging, accessible, purposeful routine to begin your math class that promotes a community of positive mathematics discussion and thinking.		5–10 minutes	NUMBER SENSE ROUTINE	
30 minutes	MATH TASK	15 minutes	FOCUS LESSON A well-planned, whole-group lesson focused on the day's learning target and accessible to all levels of learners.		45 minutes	GUIDED MATH	LEARNING STATIONS
		30 minutes	GUIDED MATH Small-group instruction that allows the teacher to support and learn more about students' understandings and misconceptions.	LEARNING STATIONS Activities in which students engage in meaningful mathematics and are provided with purposeful choices.			
20–25 minutes	TASK SHARE WITH STUDENT REFLECTION	5–10 minutes	STUDENT REFLECTION A deliberate and meaningful time for students to consider new learning.		5–10 minutes	STUDENT REFLECTION	

The Focus Lesson, Guided Math, and Learning Stations structure opens with a number sense routine, just like the other two math workshop structures begin. This routine engages all learners, promoting discourse, respect, and risk taking (see Chapter 6 for more on number sense routines). However, then, instead of a task, students engage in a focus lesson. The teacher thoughtfully and purposefully facilitates the focus lesson, limiting it to fifteen minutes or less in order to ensure it remains focused and specific. Following the focus lesson, students either collaborate in learning stations (see Chapter 7) or meet with the teacher in a guided math group (see Chapter 8). The class concludes with a reflection (see Chapter 9).

Why Use Focus Lesson, Guided Math, and Learning Stations?

The Focus Lesson, Guided Math, and Learning Stations structure is an excellent structure to use for two scenarios:

- when introducing a new topic in mathematics, and
- when introducing a new learning station.

While it is not necessary to do a focus lesson for the whole class every day, it is a good idea to do one whenever you are introducing a new math topic. As we've learned, the math workshop model is ideal for problem-based instruction. This structure allows problem-based instruction to happen during the focus lesson.

When Should I Use Focus Lesson, Guided Math, and Learning Stations?

The Focus Lesson, Guided Math, and Learning Stations structure can be used several times in a unit. When students are learning a new mathematical idea—one that was not taught in previous years—this is the structure to use. For example, students begin to explore decimals in the fourth grade. Therefore, a teacher is able to anticipate that few students will come to fourth grade with a solid understanding of decimals. So, to introduce the unit on decimals, the teacher uses this structure.

A focus lesson may or may not happen in a whole-group setting each day. As the teacher, you should make that decision based on your answer to the key question: *For how many students is this lesson appropriate?* If the answer is a small portion of your class, you should instead provide the focus lesson during guided math groups, tailoring the lesson to the needs of the group.

This is also a great structure to use when a new activity or game needs to be introduced as part of the learning stations. Using the focus lesson in this structure to introduce the new activity ensures that all students are ready for the activity when it appears in the learning stations.

What Should I Keep in Mind When Selecting a Focus Lesson?

Here are a few rules of thumb I've learned to make the most of your focus lesson in this structure:

- **Plan focus lessons based on the grade-level standards.** What is the learning target for the day? The focus lesson should be directly linked to the day's learning target. Ensure that all students find the vocabulary of the target accessible and understandable.

- **Don't show your way over and over.** As teachers we might find ourselves showing students the way we do it, and repeating this until we feel that the majority of our students understand. Remember, our way is not necessarily the best way for all of our students. As teachers we should refrain from showing our way and instead create an environment where multiple ways to solve problems are encouraged and respected. This can be a big shift for many in mathematics instruction, but this shift alone can significantly help move students forward in their conceptual understanding.

- **Use the focus lesson as a time to explore rather than tell.** Exploring the ideas of number and computation is much more powerful than telling students to memorize the algorithm. You might recall learning "Dad, Mom, Sister, Brother" to remember the steps of long division (Divide, Multiply, Subtract, Bring down). However, how many of us really understood the algorithm and how it works within the place-value system?

- **Focus on student talk more than teacher talk.** Even in the focus lesson, students should be talking more than the teacher. Remember, the person doing the most talking is likely the person doing the most learning. You don't want that to be you as the teacher; rather, ask more questions and give fewer answers. When I first started math workshop, keeping my "lips zipped" was challenging. To change this, instead of repeatedly showing my way until students "got it," I transitioned to a "less of me and more of them" mentality. That meant recognizing and following two rules: (1) I watched the time; often I set a timer to help keep the lesson at fifteen minutes. This made me more aware of when I was talking, and helped me realize that just being louder and slower does not improve student comprehension; and (2) I asked more questions; instead of "stealing students' struggle" by giving answers, I switched to probing their thinking and encouraging exploration.

- **Use talk moves.** These moves, first introduced in this resource in Chapter 2, help students stay engaged, reason, make connections, respect others' thinking, and respond to others' ideas.

- **Limit the focus lesson to fifteen minutes.** A focus lesson is often called a minilesson because it is supposed to be short and specific. Many of us as teachers struggle to cut our focus lesson down to fifteen minutes, though student engagement decreases after that time. If you struggle with keeping your focus lesson under fifteen minutes, think about what you're hoping to achieve that day—are you trying to cram in too much? Take a step back and think about the big ideas in mathematics. If needed, break the lesson into two parts—one that can be done today and one to accomplish tomorrow. Consider setting a timer so that you are aware of how much time is left in the lesson. After fifteen minutes, get students into small groups and allow them to explore the mathematics through learning stations.

- **Ensure transitions to learning stations are efficient and smooth.** Refer to Minilesson 12 in Chapter 2 to help students with transitions between learning stations.

What Does Focus Lesson, Guided Math, and Learning Stations Look Like in a Lesson?

Let's look at this structure in a lesson. (See Figure 4–1.) For a blank template to support you in creating your own Focus Lesson, Guided Math, and Learning Stations plan, see Reproducible 3.

See Reproducible 3 for a Math Workshop Lesson Plan template to help you plan a Focus Lesson, Guided Math, and Learning Stations.

Math Workshop Lesson Plan: Focus Lesson, Guided Math, and Learning Stations

Date:	Big Idea:

Number Sense Routine:

Focus Lesson:

Learning Stations:		Guided Math Groups:	Who?	What?

Student Reflection:

Reproducible 3. Math Workshop Lesson Plan: Focus Lesson, Guided Math, and Learning Stations (blank)

TIME	COMPONENT	WHAT DOES IT LOOK LIKE AND SOUND LIKE?	WHY DO IT?
5–10 minutes	Number Sense Routine: *Build It*	Ask students to show the number 6 by using their fingers. Then ask them to consider how they might show 25. Explain that they can only use fingers (no toes) and that they have to show 25 fingers. However, assure them that they can use their friends' fingers. Questions to consider asking: *–What is the largest number we could build in the room?* *–What is the largest number you could build with your friends at your table?* *–How many people would you need to build the number 52?* Ask students to build a few numbers: 38, 53, and 97. This can be done as the whole class, or ask a group of students to be the "teacher" in doing so.	It is important to start each class period together as a whole group. This promotes a sense of community. Students should be encouraged to talk in the first five minutes of the class period, be engaged in the learning, and have a positive experience. There are many number sense routines that can be used as a warm-up. See Chapter 6 for more ideas. Look for something that is engaging, purposeful, and accessible by all students. This number sense routine is anchored in the base ten system. Students strengthen their understanding of place value as they build numbers. They are also exposed to an authentic reason for skip-counting, as they count, using their fingers, by fives and tens.
15 minutes	Focus Lesson	 Show this picture to students. Pose the question: *What number could we write to tell how many we have?* Have students whisper the answer to their partner before sharing as a class. Then ask: • *How many hundreds do we have in this number?* • *How many tens do we have?* • *How many ones do we have?*	Focus lessons are intended to support the learning target of the day. These focus lessons, when done with the whole group, are student-centered and generate academic discourse. Students share their thoughts, make sense of the mathematics, and challenge conjectures.

Figure 4–1. What a Focus Lesson, Guided Math, and Learning Stations structure might look and sound like in a lesson

TIME	COMPONENT	WHAT DOES IT LOOK LIKE AND SOUND LIKE?	WHY DO IT?
		Anticipate that most students will say 1 hundred, 2 tens, and 6 ones. Challenge groups of students to create the number. Give some groups only ones cubes, others tens, and ones to yet others. Pose the questions again: • *How many hundreds?* • *How many tens?* • *How many ones?* As students create the number using ones and tens, observe whether they begin to notice that the number 126 is made up of 12 tens and 6 ones or 126 ones. If there is time remaining, provide students with another number: 307. Ask similar questions: • *How many hundreds?* • *Tens?* • *Ones?*	
30 minutes	Guided Math	Decide which students should be in each of your guided math groups; use this time to address the unique needs of these students.	Guided math time provides teachers with the opportunity to learn more about students' understandings and misconceptions. The teacher can meet with these groups for anywhere from five minutes to fifteen minutes. The quantity of time is not as important as the quality of the time. See Chapter 8 for more about guided math groups.

Figure 4–1. *(Continued)*

(continued)

TIME	COMPONENT	WHAT DOES IT LOOK LIKE AND SOUND LIKE?	WHY DO IT?
	Learning Stations	While the teacher meets with certain students for guided math, the remaining students work collaboratively and independently on activities that support their new learning and/or spiral back to other big ideas in mathematics.	Learning stations promote collaboration around engaging mathematics activities. Learning stations offer students choice and provide for differentiation. Learning stations that are meaningful and fun move students forward mathematically and ensure a positive classroom culture. See Chapter 7 for more about learning stations.
5–10 minutes	Student Reflection	Bring students back together as a whole class and ask them to reflect on and demonstrate their learning as the class discusses solving the following task: • Using the numbers 1, 2, and 3, what is the largest number you can make? • What is the smallest number you can make? • Record these numbers in your journal. Explain how many ones, tens, and hundreds are in each of the numbers. How do you know? Share your new learning with a partner.	Reflection is a deliberate and meaningful time for students to consider new learning. This opportunity is an integral part of the structure of the lesson in order to ensure that students are making meaning. See Chapter 9 for more on student reflections.

Figure 4–1. (Continued)

Math Workshop Look-Fors

If you are an administrator observing math workshop and considering what you should be looking for, or if you are a classroom teacher and wish to reflect on your own practice and do a self-assessment, you might consider using the "Look Fors" reproducible (Reproducible 4) for the Focus Lesson, Guided Math, and Learning Stations structure.

Math Workshop Look-Fors: Focus Lesson, Guided Math, and Learning Stations

Whether you are an administrator going into classrooms and needing to know what to look for when it comes to math workshop or a teacher who is reflecting on your own practice and doing self-assessment, this "Look-Fors" list will help as you consider what should be happening in this structure.

FOCUS LESSON, GUIDED MATH, AND LEARNING STATIONS

5–10 minutes	**NUMBER SENSE ROUTINE** ❏ Routine is engaging. ❏ Student discourse is happening. ❏ Routine is accessible to all students.
15 minutes	**FOCUS LESSON** ❏ Teacher has a reason for holding a whole-group focus lesson. ❏ Lesson is well-planned. ❏ There is student discourse (talk). ❏ Teacher uses talk moves.
30 minutes	**GUIDED MATH** ❏ Teacher meets with groups of students. ❏ Lessons are purposeful and differentiated for each group. ❏ Teacher takes anecdotal records (notes). ❏ Teacher asks thoughtful questions.	**LEARNING STATIONS** Evidence that students know: ❏ where to go ❏ what to do ❏ how to transition Activities are: ❏ engaging ❏ mathematically purposeful ❏ accessible
5–10 minutes	**STUDENT REFLECTION** ❏ Students share learning for the day and/or ❏ Students share strategies and/or ❏ Students write about their learning and/or ❏ Students complete an exit ticket or other formative assessment

Reproducible 4. Math Workshop Look-Fors: Focus Lesson, Guided Math, and Learning Stations

See Reproducible 4 for "look fors" for Focus Lesson, Guided Math, and Learning Stations.

Connecting the Chapter to Your Practice

- How does what you currently do in your classroom connect to the components of a Focus Lesson, Guided Math, and Learning Stations structure?

- What is your vision of a math workshop at this point? How does the Focus Lesson, Guided Math, and Learning Stations structure fit with that vision? In what ways does it not?

- What do your focus lessons currently look like? How are students engaged? How are the needs of all students being met?

- What changes would you make to your focus lesson in order for each lesson to be fifteen minutes in length and more student-centered?

- As you consider your upcoming unit, how might you use the Focus Lesson, Guided Math, and Learning Stations structure of math workshop in it?

 VIDEO CLIP 4.1 ·

The Focus Lesson, Guided Math, and Learning Stations Structure in Action, Revisited

Rewatch this clip, bringing the insights you've learned from this chapter into play. Consider the following question:

- What do you notice in this clip since watching it the first time and reading this chapter?

To view this video clip, scan the QR code or access via mathsolutions.com/mathworkshop41

Guided Math and Learning Stations Structure

CHAPTER 5

VIDEO CLIP 5.1 ·

The Guided Math and Learning Stations Structure in Action

This clip highlights excerpts from Ms. Wallace's first-grade class as she facilitates a Guided Math and Learning Stations math workshop structure. As you watch this clip, consider these questions:

- What math workshop characteristics do you see happening in this video (see Chapter 1, page 4, Seven Math Workshop Characteristics)?
- What do you notice about what is happening in the guided math groups? How is this similar to and different from what is happening in the learning stations?
- What surprises you about this way of doing math workshop?
- How is what is happening in this classroom different or similar to what is happening in your classroom?
- What questions might you have after watching this clip?

To view this video clip, scan the QR code or access via mathsolutions.com/mathworkshop51

· ·

What Is *Guided Math and Learning Stations?*

MATH WORKSHOP: TASK AND SHARE		MATH WORKSHOP: FOCUS LESSON, GUIDED MATH, AND LEARNING STATIONS			MATH WORKSHOP: GUIDED MATH AND LEARNING STATIONS		
5 minutes	NUMBER SENSE ROUTINE	5–10 minutes	NUMBER SENSE ROUTINE		5–10 minutes	NUMBER SENSE ROUTINE An engaging, accessible, purposeful routine to begin your math class that promotes a community of positive mathematics discussion and thinking.	
30 minutes	MATH TASK	15 minutes	FOCUS LESSON		45 minutes	GUIDED MATH Small-group instruction that allows the teacher to support and learn more about students' understandings and misconceptions. In this structure, the focus lesson is addressed in guided math groups.	LEARNING STATIONS Activities in which students engage in meaningful mathematics and are provided with purposeful choices.
		30 minutes	GUIDED MATH	LEARNING STATIONS			
20–25 minutes	TASK SHARE WITH STUDENT REFLECTION	5–10 minutes	STUDENT REFLECTION		5–10 minutes	STUDENT REFLECTION A deliberate and meaningful time for students to consider new learning.	

The Guided Math and Learning Stations structure opens with a number sense routine, just like the other two math workshop structures begin. This routine engages all learners, promoting discourse, respect, and risk taking (see Chapter 6 for more on number sense routines). However, then, instead of a task or whole-class focus lesson, students immediately engage in learning stations and/or guided math groups. The focus lesson still occurs, but it happens within the guided math groups. The class concludes with a reflection (see Chapter 9 for more on reflections).

Why Use Guided Math and Learning Stations?

There are so many times I've looked out over the sea of students in my classroom and thought, *If I could just get each of you all to myself, even for a little bit, I could focus on what you really need.* However, that kind of individual attention takes time. The Guided Math and Learning Stations structure is meant to give teachers the class time needed to work with small groups or individual students. By removing the whole-group focus lesson, time is freed up to focus on and use the lesson in guided math groups.

When Should I Use Guided Math and Learning Stations?

The Guided Math and Learning Stations structure is best used in two scenarios:

- when a whole-class focus lesson has already been done on the mathematical topic (this might have been as recently as yesterday). As the teacher you do not need to share anything else new (related to the topic) with the whole group, and you are most interested in reaching students through small groups to see where their thinking resides on the topic; and

- when data shows that any amount of time spent speaking to the whole group will most likely only impact a small portion of students. For example, you are about to work on the topic of money with students. You have given a pretest, and you see the following:

  - five of your students are not yet able to identify the coins;

  - six students can identify the coins by their characteristics, but they are not able to identify the value of the coins;

- four of your students are able to count sets of coins as long as the coin is the same, but they are not yet able to count mixed sets of coins;
- five students can count mixed sets of coins, but they are not yet able to make change from a dollar; and
- two students can make change from a dollar.

In this situation, it is best to get these students into small groups and have more time with them. Your focus lesson will be much more effective when it is differentiated for various small groups of students during guided math instruction.

What Should I Keep in Mind When Forming Guided Math Groups?

Guided math groups are often more fluid than in reading. This is something that many teachers find to be different from guided reading groups. Typically, guided reading groups may stay intact for a longer time frame. In math, however, a group of students that the teacher puts together on Monday may not be together for Tuesday's group. All guided math groups are formed with the understanding that they are temporary and can change frequently (see the lesson at the end of this chapter for an example of how groups might change). It is important to use both heterogeneous and homogeneous groups, exposing students to groups that may be based on interest and not always instructional needs. See Chapter 8 for a more in-depth look at guided math groups, including three ways to best group students: readiness, heterogeneous, or random grouping.

As stated previously, in this structure the focus lesson is addressed in guided math groups. However, whether the focus lesson is being done in a small, guided math group or in a whole group, it is important to remember the rules of thumb that are stated in Chapter 4 (page 123). In a nutshell, encourage students to show their strategies; allow time for exploration; promote the use of student talk and talk moves; and limit your lesson (even in guided math groups) to no more than fifteen minutes.

Also refer back to the discussion on small groups in Chapter 1 (page 16). Buffum, Mattos, and Weber (2009) explain that differentiating instruction and small-group activities are the most important steps that a school can make to improve the core instruction. Small guided math groups provide students with the opportunity for "just-right" math instruction and the opportunity to problem solve with their peers. In guided math groups, teachers gather an abundance of information on each student, something that can be overwhelmingly difficult when faced with trying to do so with a whole class. The teacher's role in guided math groups is to ask questions that provide insights into students' thinking. In guided math groups, teachers get to know a student's readiness level, approach to tasks, learning preferences/styles, the vocabulary that students possess, and what students connect to in real life and previous mathematics. Teachers, during guided math instruction, are evaluating student understanding, taking anecdotal notes, and making mental notes about future grouping possibilities.

What Is Considered a Small Group?

The size of a small group may vary. During guided math, I might be working with four students. Or eight. Or even one. Group size is not something that I spend too much time worrying about. I usually shoot for a group of four or five. However, sometimes, according to the data or the lesson itself, it makes sense to have the group be a bit bigger or smaller. Just like in reading workshop, some groups are going to be larger than others. These group sizes may be different even from day to day.

The thing to remember is that, in math workshop, all groups that are formed for instruction are temporary and should be changed frequently. It is important to use both heterogeneous and homogeneous groups, exposing students to groups that may be based on interest and not always instructional needs. Groups are put together thoughtfully and intentionally. See Chapter 1 (page 16) for more insight on small groups.

What Does Guided Math and Learning Stations Look Like in a Lesson?

Let's look at this structure in a lesson. (See Figure 5–1.) For a blank template to support you in creating your own Guided Math and Learning Stations, see Reproducible 5.

See Reproducible 5 for a Math Workshop Lesson Plan template to help you plan Guided Math and Learning Stations.

Math Workshop Lesson Plan: Guided Math and Learning Stations

Date:		Big Idea:		
Number Sense Routine:				
Learning Stations:		Guided Math Groups:	Who?	What?
Student Reflection:				

Reproducible 5. Math Workshop Lesson Plan: Guided Math and Learning Stations (blank)

TIME	COMPONENT	WHAT DOES IT LOOK LIKE AND SOUND LIKE?	WHY DO IT?
5–10 minutes	Number Sense Routine: *Count Around*	Have students sit in a circle on the floor. If space does not allow, this can be done with students at their seats. Tell students that you are going to count around the circle or room by tens. Before you start counting, ask students to consider what number they believe the last student will say. Have them whisper this to their partner.	It is important to start each class period together as a whole group. This promotes a sense of community. Students should be encouraged to talk in the first five minutes or so of the class period, be engaged in the learning, and have a positive experience. There are many number sense routines that can be used to begin your math class. See Chapter 6 for more ideas. Look for something that is engaging, purposeful, and accessible to all students.
		Other questions to consider: • *If we count around by fives, what would the last person say?* • *Is there a place in the counting that we might get stuck? If so, where might it be?* Allow time for students to share with their partners. After the counting, return to the questions; affirm predictions.	The routine *count around* was purposefully chosen for this lesson because of the connection to counting money. Connecting counting money to skip-counting may help students later in the lesson.
45 minutes	Guided Math Groups	Decide which students should be in each of your guided math groups; use this time to address the unique needs of these students (see Figure 5–2 on page 139 for the suggested guided math groups based on the preassessment).	Guided math time provides teachers with the opportunity to learn more about students' understandings and misconceptions. The teacher can meet with these groups anywhere from five minutes to fifteen minutes. The quantity of time is not as important as the quality of the time. See Chapter 8 for more about guided math groups.

Figure 5–1. What a Guided Math and Learning Stations structure might look and sound like in a lesson

(continued)

TIME	COMPONENT	WHAT DOES IT LOOK LIKE AND SOUND LIKE?	WHY DO IT?
	Learning Stations	While the teacher meets with certain students for guided math, the remaining students work at learning stations, collaboratively and independently, on activities that support their new learning and/or spiral back to other big ideas in mathematics.	Learning stations promote collaboration around engaging mathematics activities. Learning stations offer students choice and provide for differentiation. Learning stations that are meaningful and fun move students forward mathematically and ensure a positive classroom culture. See Chapter 7 for more about learning stations.
5–10 minutes	Student Reflection	Find a partner that you did not work with in a learning station today. Tell that partner two things: 1. What is one piece of new learning you had today? 2. What was your favorite learning station today and why?	Reflection is a deliberate and meaningful time for students to consider new learning. This opportunity is an integral part of the structure of the lesson in order to ensure that students are making meaning.

Figure 5–1. *(Continued)*

Remember, you don't need to meet with each of these groups for the same amount of time. Fair isn't always equal. For example, you may meet with Group 2 for 10 minutes, meet with Group 3 for 15 minutes, and meet with Group 5 for 8 minutes. This kind of flexibility allows you to meet with all students and provide them with "just-right" instruction. Also keep in mind that your list of groups is a private one. It should never be displayed for students to see.

These groups are fluid and could easily change in one day. However, let's say that the teacher planned for the groups that are listed in Figure 5–2 and met with them. The teacher found out some very important information that he acts on as follows:

- Fabian and Nia were able to identify coins rather quickly. The teacher has decided to put them into the group that is working to identify the value of the coins.

- Faith, Dakota, and Gabe have shown that they can identify the value of the coins, so the teacher decides to pull them into a new group to see if they can count same coin sets (a set of nickels, a set of dimes, a set of pennies).

- Nadia seemed to struggle with making change. The teacher gave her a set of mixed coins, and she struggled. The teacher decides to move her to Group 3 tomorrow to support her with this need.
- Adib was flying through the lesson and making change from $1 with no problem. The teacher decides to see how Adib does with Aidan and Madie tomorrow.

The list of guided groups has now changed; see Figure 5–3.

GROUP 1	GROUP 2	GROUP 3	GROUP 4	GROUP 5
Identifying Coins	Value of Coins	Counting Mixed Sets	Making Change from $1	Extending to $5
Fabian	Abbey	Nadeen	Aisley	Aidan
Omar	Faith	Sam	Nadia	Madie
Nia	Dakota	Raamiz	Mitchell	
Avery	Gabe	Raffael	Adib	
Landon	Nathan		Nahomi	
	Eric			

Figure 5–2. Guided math groups, Version 1

GROUP 1	GROUP 2	NEW GROUP	GROUP 3	GROUP 4	GROUP 5
Identifying Coins	Value of Coins	Count Same Coin Sets	Counting Mixed Sets	Making Change from $1	Extending to $5
~~Fabian~~	Abbey	Faith	Nadeen	Aisley	Aidan
Omar	~~Faith~~	Dakota	Sam	~~Nadia~~	Madie
~~Nia~~	~~Dakota~~	Gabe	Raamiz	Mitchell	Adib
Avery	~~Gabe~~		Raffael	~~Adib~~	
Landon	Nathan		Nadia	Nahomi	
	Eric				
	Fabian				
	Nia				

Figure 5–3. Guided math groups, Version 2

Math Workshop Look-Fors

If you are an administrator observing math workshop and considering what you should be looking for, or if you are a classroom teacher and wish to reflect on your own practice and do a self-assessment, you might consider using the "Look Fors" reproducible (Reproducible 6) for the Guided Math and Learning Stations structure.

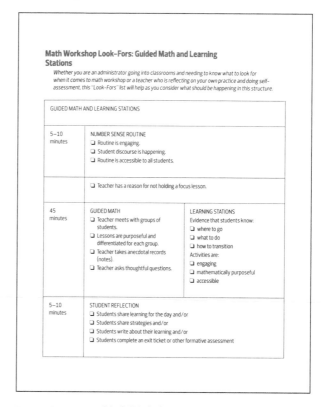

See Reproducible 6 for "look fors" for Guided Math and Learning Stations.

Reproducible 6. Math Workshop Look-Fors: Guided Math and Learning Stations

Connecting the Chapter to Your Practice

- How does what you currently do in your classroom connect to the components of a Guided Math and Learning Stations structure?

- Consider a lesson that you taught to your whole class that was too difficult for some students and too easy for others. How might that lesson have transpired differently using the Guided Math and Learning Stations structure?

- How do you already use data to inform your lesson decisions? How might you use that data to decide which lessons to teach the whole class and which lessons to teach in guided math groups?

- What are some topics in your grade level that you find to have the greatest range of need? How might you facilitate student understanding of these topics using the Guided Math and Learning Stations structure?

- How do you currently take notes on student progress, understanding, and strategies during mathematics? Is that system working for you? If not, how might your modify your system to make it more user-friendly?

- As you consider your upcoming unit, how might you use the Guided Math and Learning Stations structure of math workshop in it?

 **VIDEO CLIP 5.1** ·

The Guided Math and Learning Stations Structure in Action, Revisited

Rewatch this clip, bringing the insights you've learned from this chapter into play. Consider the following question:

- What do you notice in this video since watching it the first time and reading this chapter?

To view this video clip, scan the QR code or access via mathsolutions.com/mathworkshop51

· ·

Facilitate Your Math Workshop

STEP 4

This section of the book focuses on the components found in each of the three structures of math workshop. By focusing on how to efficiently and effectively facilitate number sense routines, learning stations, guided math groups, and student reflections, your confidence in putting these together in a full math class will grow. Even if you are hesitant to jump into significant change in your system of mathematics instruction, this section will support you in adopting at least one of the components. Perhaps you simply want to make a shift in how you begin or end your class; if so, you might want to go right to Chapter 6 ("Number Sense Routine") and Chapter 9 ("Student Reflection"). Basically, take on what you can, and use this book as your support as you embark on this change—as little or as big as it may be.

. . . .

Chapters in Step 4

Number Sense Routine

What Is a Number Sense Routine?

A number sense routine is an engaging, accessible, purposeful routine to begin your math class that promotes a community of positive mathematics discussion and thinking.

MATH WORKSHOP: TASK AND SHARE		MATH WORKSHOP: FOCUS LESSON, GUIDED MATH, AND LEARNING STATIONS			MATH WORKSHOP: GUIDED MATH AND LEARNING STATIONS		
5–10 minutes	NUMBER SENSE ROUTINE	5–10 minutes	NUMBER SENSE ROUTINE		5–10 minutes	NUMBER SENSE ROUTINE	
30 minutes	MATH TASK	15 minutes	FOCUS LESSON		45 minutes	GUIDED MATH	LEARNING STATIONS
		30 minutes	GUIDED MATH	LEARNING STATIONS			
20–25 minutes	TASK SHARE WITH STUDENT REFLECTION	5–10 minutes	STUDENT REFLECTION		5–10 minutes	STUDENT REFLECTION	

A number sense routine is students' first impression of mathematics for the day; make it a good one! Several ideas for number sense routines are provided in the last part of this chapter—you might be familiar with some of them, such as *Which one doesn't belong?*, *number of the day*, and *number talks*.

Why Use a Number Sense Routine?

Early in my teaching career I did not see the value of a warm-up. To me it was simply something to keep students busy while I gained the necessary transition time to move from one content area to the next. In addition, when I assigned a warm-up, often a handful of students finished almost immediately while others rarely got started; the warm-up was only hitting about one-third of my students—and yet, it was my students' first impression of mathematics for the day. I started to realize how influential a warm-up could be on students' learning; a child who cannot access the mathematics or is not engaged in the first five minutes of class could quite possibly shut down for the next fifty-five minutes or, worse yet, the whole year. On the other hand, a child who gets talking and is actively engaged right away is more likely to share their thinking throughout the rest of the lesson—and year. I made a commitment to not dismiss these first few minutes as simply transitional time and started using number sense routines. In doing so I saw a significant change in students' engagement during the lesson, flexibility with numbers, respect for various problem-solving strategies, positivity toward mathematics, and willingness to take risks. I was hooked!

When Should I Use a Number Sense Routine?

Regardless of which of the three math workshop structures you choose (see Chapters 3–5), you should always start off the first five to ten minutes with a number sense routine. As you first attempt number sense routines, try not to be discouraged by students who are hesitant to share; this is certainly not a reason to stop using routines in class. Remember that this may be a shift for you, and it may also be a shift for your students. Give it time.

What Does a Number Sense Routine
Look Like During Math Workshop?

Number sense routines don't have to look exactly the same each and every day. However, to make them "routine," it is important to do them consistently. Following are ideas for number sense routines that I've found to be most effective in increasing student engagement, encouraging student discourse, and creating (as well as sustaining) a sense of community. Not to mention they're fun!

Ideas for Number Sense Routines

- *Which one doesn't belong?*
- *number of the day*
- *number talk*
- *count around*
- *finger patterns*
- *building numbers*

Which One Doesn't Belong?

The *Which one doesn't belong?* routine encourages everyone's ideas to be heard; no answers are considered "wrong." Many students for whom mathematics has been a struggle or who already have a negative disposition toward mathematics will find comfort in this routine if facilitated in the appropriate way.

When I first introduce this routine I typically start with items that have very little or nothing to do with numbers at all. This is important so that students see how the routine works and are more open to sharing their thoughts out loud. You might start off by showing all students the following:

Which One Doesn't Belong?

Students might say:

- *The zebra doesn't belong because it is not something that I see often.*
- *The beetle doesn't belong because the zebra and the dog each have four legs but the beetle does not.*
- *The dog doesn't belong because the zebra and the beetle each have black on it.*

The possibilities you might hear from a group of imaginative students are endless—and you might even find that it's challenging to get students to stop thinking of possibilities! Here are six steps that I've found helpful in keeping the routine on track—and limited to five to ten minutes:

1. Show students a set of three images, numbers, etc. Ask them, "Which one doesn't belong? Why?" Give students a minute of individual think time.

2. Ask students to turn and talk to a partner. Have them explain to each other which does not belong and why.

3. Bring the class back together. Ask a student to share an interesting thought that they heard from their partner or a thought of their own.

4. When the student shares the response, paraphrase their answer back to them and refrain from showing any judgment or favoritism of any kind. Thank the student for sharing.

5. Ask, "Who thought of it the same way?" Take hands or a "me too" signal.

6. Ask, "What's a different way someone thought about it?" Continue this process until you believe you either have exhausted all ideas or need to move on.

Why facilitate this routine in this way? The teacher moves used here are important. By giving students individual think time, you ensure all students will have an answer to share with their partner. By providing time to talk to a partner, you make certain all voices in the room are heard, even if you don't have time to call on each student to share. You are also giving students time to practice what they might share with the whole group. When paraphrasing student responses, you use this as an opportunity to insert mathematical vocabulary that may not be used by the student. By not showing favoritism or judgment, you send the message that all answers are encouraged and that you do not have one particular answer in mind that you are looking for. By closely following the six steps, more students will be willing to share and take risks. Simple moves to make, right? Simple, yet critical to building community in your classroom. You are reinforcing that in your classroom, everyone has different ideas and all ideas are respected.

Once students understand how this routine works, they will start to feel confident that as the teacher you really are open to all ideas, and their idea will not be judged. When this happens, bring in a number example such as:

Which One Doesn't Belong?

5   10   4

Depending on the grade level, you might get answers like:

- *The 5 does not belong because it is odd and the other two are even.*
- *The 4 does not belong because it is not a factor of 10.*
- *The 10 does not belong because it is a two-digit number and the other two have only one digit.*

Number of the Day

Number of the day is a simple routine that takes very little preparation on behalf of the teacher. Simply choose a number (the "number of the day") and ask students to come up with as many ways to make/show that number as possible. Students will start to think more flexibly about numbers, recognize ways to decompose numbers, and realize that they don't have to use a number as it is when performing computation. Caution: though this is called *number of the day*, I recommend not using it every day—it is good to switch up your number sense routines to keep students engaged.

Let's consider the number 10 as the "number of the day" and walk through what this might look like in several grade levels:

Kindergarten

The number 10 as number of the day in a kindergarten class provides the most wonderful responses. Students may draw pictures of ten items. They may show as many combinations of ten as they can come up with: 5 and 5, 1 and 9, etc.

Grade 3

The number 10 as the number of the day in a third-grade classroom provides just as wonderful a response. Students might use all of the operations to come up with ways to make 10, such as $8 + 2$, $20 - 10$, 5×2, and $20 \div 2$. They may even use more than two numbers, such as $4 + 4 + 2$. Or, they use more than one operation, such as $8 - 2 + 4$.

Grade 5

The number 10 as the number of the day in a fifth-grade classroom could instigate responses that bring about discussions of the properties; order of operations; decimals; fractions; and positive and negative integers. Just because you are dealing with an upper grade, does not mean that the number needs to get bigger. The math just gets deeper!

With this routine, the possibilities are endless and the thinking is fabulous. The conversations are rich in mathematics and best of all—every single student in the classroom can participate in this activity. A student who has struggled before in mathematics may come up with one or two ideas to start, while another student may make a list of twenty combinations within minutes.

Number Talk

A *number talk* is a five- to fifteen-minute classroom conversation around purposefully crafted computation problems that are solved mentally (Parrish 2010, 2014). That is right—no paper or pencil! In a nutshell, to facilitate a number talk, purposefully select a problem, write it where all students can see it, have students mentally solve it, then engage students in a conversation in which they share their strategies for solving it. Here are examples of students' mental math strategies that you might see using the problem 38 + 25:

38 + 25		
Sean	**Darnell**	**Jayden**
38 + 25 30 + 20 = 50 8 + 5 = 13 50 + 13 = 63	38 + 25 30 + 20 = 50 8 + 2 = 10 *("I used only 2 of the 5 to make another 10.")* 50 + 10 = 60 60 + 3 = 63	38 + 25 30 + 20 = 50 50 + 8 = 58 58 + 5 = 63
Claire	**Liam**	**Sophia**
38 + 25 38 + 20 = 58 58 + 2 *("from the 5")* = 60 60 + 3 = 63 *("Because I still had 3 from the 5.")*	38 + 25 38 + 2 = 40 *("I took 2 from the 25 and gave it to the 38.")* 40 + 23 *("that left me with only 23 to add")* = 63	38 + 25 40 + 25 = 65 *("I made the 38 a 40 because it was easier.")* 65 − 2 = 63 *("I had to take 2 off since I added 2 to the 38.")*

If you're interested in doing number talks in your classroom as part of your number sense routines, I highly recommend *Number Talks: Whole Number Computation* (2010, 2014) by Sherry Parrish and *Number Talks: Fractions, Decimals, and Percentages* by Sherry Parrish and Ann Dominck (2016). In each book, the author(s) explains the value of such a routine, provides many examples of number strings at various grade levels, and includes videos of number talks happening in classrooms.

 **VIDEO CLIP 6.1**

Number Sense Routine: Number Talk Using Quick Images

In this clip Ms. Wallace, to start math workshop with her first graders, chooses to do a number sense routine in the form of a number talk using quick images. As you watch this clip, consider the following questions:

- What math workshop characteristics do you see happening in this video (see Chapter 1, page 4, Seven Math Workshop Characteristics)?
- How does this number sense routine support flexibility with numbers?
- Do you use number talks in your classroom? If so, in what ways? If not, what is a number talk that you would you like to try with your students?

To see how the rest of Ms. Wallace's math workshop unfolds after this routine, refer to Video Clip 5.1.

To view this video clip, scan the QR code or access via mathsolutions.com/mathworkshop61

Count Around

A *count around* is a routine that takes very little time and gets every student talking within the first few minutes of class. However they "count around," students are listening to each other and anticipating the numbers that will come next. They know that their turn will come (and possibly come back again), so they pay close attention to every number that is being said out loud. Let's look at how this routine might unfold at various grade levels:

Kindergarten

Kindergartners sit in a circle. As the teacher I ask them to start counting at one and count up to thirty. Or I might ask them to start at thirty and count backward.

Grade 3

In a third-grade classroom in which students are exploring multiplication, I might ask them to practice skip-counting around the room by threes or fours to help reinforce the concept of multiples.

Grade 5

In a fifth-grade classroom, I might ask students to count forward by one-fourths.

Great questions to ask students when using a count around as a number sense routine might include the following:

- If we are counting by ones and we start here at Jenna, what number do you think the last person will say?
- What number will the person say that is halfway around the circle?
- Where might we get stuck as we count?
- If we are counting by fives around the room, do you think we will ever say the number one hundred?

 **VIDEO CLIP 6.2** ·

Number Sense Routine: Count Around

In this clip, we see a number sense routine—count around—happening in two classrooms that are using it to begin math workshop: first in Ms. Griswold's kindergarten class and then in Ms. Hrabak's fourth-grade class. As you watch this clip, consider the following questions:

- What math workshop characteristics do you see happening in this video (see Chapter 1, page 4, Seven Math Workshop Characteristics)?
- Do you use count arounds in your classroom? If so, in what ways? If not, what is a count around that you would you like to try with your students?

To see how the rest of Ms. Hrabak's math workshop unfolds after this routine, refer to Video Clip 4.1.

To view this video clip, scan the QR code or access via mathsolutions.com/mathworkshop62

· ·

Finger Patterns

Finger patterns, also referred to as *show me*, is a number sense routine that is typically done in the primary grades and takes very little preparation. It focuses on decomposing numbers using fingers. I start off by having all students hold their hands up in fists to indicate *zero*:

Then I ask students to show the number 1. I do this to ensure that they only put up one finger versus one finger on each hand:

Then I ask them to show me a number, such as the number 6. I may see students who, with their fingers, are showing me a combination of 5 and 1, or 4 and 2, or 3 and 3. I then ask them to show me 6 *another* way. I might stop and ask them to look at their friends. *Look at all the ways that our friends have shown six.*

We continue to do this with a few other numbers. During this activity, I'm on the lookout for students who need to count each finger as they put it up or those who struggle with moving on to the second hand. Not only does this routine engage students and help them think more flexibly about numbers, but it provides me a lot of information about them!

VIDEO CLIP 6.3 ·

Number Sense Routine: Finger Patterns

In this clip Ms. Wallace, to start math workshop with her first graders, facilitates a number sense routine, finger patterns. As you watch this video clip, consider the following questions:

- What math workshop characteristics do you see happening in this clip (see Chapter 1, page 4, Seven Math Workshop Characteristics)?

- How does this number sense routine support flexibility with numbers?

To view this video clip, scan the QR code or access via mathsolutions.com/mathworkshop63

· ·

Building Numbers

Building numbers is a routine that I like to use with grades K–3. It takes little to no prep time. It is very similar to the finger patterns routine in that students are asked to create numbers using their fingers. However, this routine moves well beyond the number 10. Here are the steps I take in facilitating this routine:

1. I start by asking students to show me a number like 7 with their fingers. I ask them, "How can we check to make sure we have seven?" We usually all agree that we could count our fingers.

2. I then ask students to build a number such as 18. The first time I do this routine, I get some pretty funny responses—especially if I do this with kindergartners or first graders. They pull off their shoes and try to use their toes in addition to their fingers; stick out their tongues; show me their eyes and ears . . . it makes me laugh every time. I explain that they must use *fingers*, but they are welcome to use more than just their *own* fingers. Their eyes start to sparkle, and they quickly get with a partner to make 18.

3. After this, I move onto larger numbers like 32, 47, or 51. As students get into groups, they are abuzz with mathematical reasoning: *How many tens—both of my hands—will I need to make this number? Do I need another friend for any leftover ones?*

4. Once students have practiced this, I calm the activity down a bit by asking one student to be my builder. I explain that only the builder can talk. I tell the builder that they must build a certain number. For example, let's say that number is 63. I ask the builder, "How many friends will you need to build the number 63?" The builder brings other students to the front of the room to build the number 63 by telling each student how many fingers to hold up. Then I ask the class how we can find out if the builder built the correct number. The class insists that we need to count. Slowly, and painfully, I begin to count by ones. Often, students are okay with this for the first number or two. However, after that, impatience sets in (indicated by huffs and puffs and eye-rolling). When I sense impatience, I ask the class if there is a faster way to count. They often offer up to skip-count by tens or fives. What a beautiful thing to arrive at a reason for skip-counting beyond just thinking we're doing it because it's in the standards!

Your questions and directions can vary as you do this routine. Consider asking students to build any number using four friends. Or ask them, "What is the largest number we could build if we used every person in the class to help?" The differentiation that can take place in this activity is limitless; depending on the number you choose and the questions you ask, you can easily change the complexity level.

Some of My Favorite Books for Number Sense Routines

- Minilessons for Math Practice series by Rusty Bresser and Caren Holtzman
- *Number Talks: Whole Number Computation* by Sherry Parrish
- *Number Talks: Fractions, Decimals, and Percentages* by Sherry Parrish and Ann Dominick
- *Number Sense Routines: Building Numerical Literacy Every Day in Grades K–3* by Jessica Shumway

Connecting the Chapter to Your Practice

- Which number sense routine listed in this chapter do you see as appropriate to begin with your students? What numbers might you use with it?
- How might you use one of these number sense routines during other parts of the day outside of math class? Is there time during morning meeting? Pack up?
- What other number sense routines do you already use that could be utilized during math workshop?

Learning Stations

(continued)

 **VIDEO CLIP 7.1** ·

The Power of Learning Stations

In this clip the author, Ms. Lempp, talks about what makes a good learning station. As you watch this clip, consider the following questions:

- What stands out to you about what Ms. Lempp describes as a good learning station?
- What do you see students doing?
- What questions do you have about learning stations as a component of math workshop?

To view this video clip, scan the QR code or access via mathsolutions.com/mathworkshop71

· ·

What Are Learning Stations?

Learning stations are activities in which students engage in meaningful mathematics and are provided with purposeful choices.

MATH WORKSHOP: TASK AND SHARE		MATH WORKSHOP: FOCUS LESSON, GUIDED MATH, AND LEARNING STATIONS			MATH WORKSHOP: GUIDED MATH AND LEARNING STATIONS		
5–10 minutes	NUMBER SENSE ROUTINE	5–10 minutes	NUMBER SENSE ROUTINE		5–10 minutes	NUMBER SENSE ROUTINE	
30 minutes	MATH TASK	15 minutes	FOCUS LESSON		45 minutes	GUIDED MATH	LEARNING STATIONS
		30 minutes	GUIDED MATH	LEARNING STATIONS			
20–25 minutes	TASK SHARE WITH STUDENT REFLECTION	5–10 minutes	STUDENT REFLECTION		5–10 minutes	STUDENT REFLECTION	

Learning stations, centers, partner games—there are several terms used to describe this component of math workshop. The words aren't as important as the quality of the activities and the intentional use of this time. Learning stations are activities in which students engage in meaningful mathematics and are provided with purposeful choices. In math workshop, students may take part in several learning stations via an organizational system (often math menus). The math workshop structures Focus Lesson, Guided Math, and Learning Stations (Chapter 4) and Guided Math and Learning Stations (Chapter 5) both use learning stations.

Why Use Learning Stations?

Learning stations are meant to enrich student understanding, promote a love of mathematics, and support student engagement so that the teacher is able to more closely monitor student learning as well as work with small guided math groups. Learning stations also make learning mathematics fun! The use of learning activities generate an excitement for the content. By approaching student learning through fun games and activities, you will engage students who otherwise would be anxious about mathematics or believe that they are not good at it. Providing students with engaging, meaningful, and enjoyable math learning stations may help break down some of the barriers that many students bring to math class.

A fourth-grade teacher once confided in me that her students were seriously struggling with fractions, and she feared that she could not move on to the next unit as a result. I recommended that she consider moving on to the next unit and add fraction stations as part of her learning station options in math workshop. She embraced the idea and implemented several different fraction stations over the next month. She also met with guided math groups alongside the stations. In just one month she remarked to me that students' fraction understanding was deepening!

When Should I Use Learning Stations?

You can start a learning station immediately; however, I recommend when first starting to stick to just one station. If your students have not been exposed to learning stations, start off with several copies or sets of the *same* learning station. The first few days should be about practice and feedback. For example, provide students with an activity—something relatively easy that doesn't take a lot of modeling to understand. I often start with a matching activity. Then remind students of the expectations and monitor them. Afterward, bring students together as a whole class to reflect on what went well and how they could improve. Provide them with feedback. The next day, you might build to two learning stations and move your focus to providing feedback on transitioning from one station activity to another. As you add more stations, continue to revisit expectations. Eventually give students the opportunity to choose their stations. When you do this, you are still not pulling guided math groups. Your time is spent monitoring these stations, reaffirming your expectations, and providing feedback. Once students are capable of working in learning stations without your strict monitoring, this is your cue to begin guided math groups as well (see Chapter 8).

The most important thing to remember about learning stations is that quality is more important than quantity. Having more options to choose from is of no value if the learning stations are not appropriate and engaging. Typically, a learning station can remain in play for a week or longer; it completely depends on the concept. There are times when you can use a station for week, take it out for a few weeks, and then add it back in. At other times, the type of station itself can stay the same (be a routine), but the topic might change. For example, a matching game can be used over and over—you can match expanded form to standard form, time on an analog clock to time on a digital clock, equivalent fractions, and so forth. Using routines in learning stations can also help decrease the time it takes to teach students what to do.

> The most important thing to remember about learning stations is that quality is more important than quantity.

 VIDEO CLIP 7.2 ....

Introducing an Activity for a Learning Station

In this clip, Ms. Robinson briefly describes how she introduces an activity for a learning station to her second graders. As you watch this clip, consider the following questions:

- What stands out to you about what Ms. Robinson does and asks when introducing an activity?

- Why do you think Ms. Robinson chooses to introduce the activity to the whole group?
- How do you introduce a new activity to your students?

To view this video clip, scan the QR code or access via mathsolutions.com/mathworkshop72

. . . .

What Should I Keep in Mind Before Learning Stations?

There are five critical steps to take before getting students actively involved in learning stations:

Step 1: Make sure the three buckets are "full."

Step 2: Create learning stations.

Step 3: Create learning station groups.

Step 4: Determine the system in which students choose their learning stations.

Step 5: Determine how students move through learning stations.

Let's take a closer look at each of these steps.

Step 1: Make Sure the Three Buckets Are "Full"

In Chapter 2, we learned about the three buckets that represent the conditions that must be in place for a successful math workshop: classroom arrangement, routines and procedures, and mathematics community. Make sure these three buckets are "full" before starting learning stations.

Bucket 1: Classroom Arrangement

Classroom arrangement is especially important in helping students answer the question *Where do I go?* Create locations that allow you to see all students from where you are seated for guided math. In addition, look at the location where students will be working from their vantage point. What is around that could distract them or keep them from being able to continue to work? Students, when working in learning stations, will often have at least one partner and could be in groups of three, four, or more. What spaces in your room can serve as places for partner and small-group work? See the discussion of the first bucket, classroom arrangement, in Chapter 2 for more on this topic.

Bucket 2: Routines and Procedures

The second bucket, routines and procedures, is critical to ensuring learning stations don't become a classroom management nightmare. Being explicit about expectations for working collaboratively; practicing those expectations with students and providing feedback to them will help them stay engaged and on task during learning stations when you are not there to directly supervise them.

For starters, when students are asked to engage in learning stations, they should easily and quickly know the answers to these questions:

- *What can I do?*
- *Where do I go?*
- *Who can I work with?*
- *How long do I do it?*
- *What do I do if I have a question?*
- *What do I do when I'm finished?*

Chapter 2 supports these questions and more. Take time as a teacher or in your grade-level team to think about these questions and what you want for the answers.

Bucket 3: Mathematics Community

A significant part of the third bucket, mathematics community, is the expectation that students are respectfully talking with each other. Imagine a learning station in which rich mathematical tasks are being discussed, worked, and reworked over and over by students. These students are all attacking a problem with their own strategy, discussing these strategies, and comparing how the strategies are similar and different. Students are debating the accuracy of each person's answer and the efficiency of each person's strategy. They are leaders of their own learning.

Don't hesitate to revisit one of the minilessons from Chapter 2 any time you find your students struggling with the expectations created by these three buckets.

Step 2: Create Learning Stations

It's critical to have learning stations that are engaging and accessible for all students. This means that teachers are not just giving students a pack of worksheets to complete at each station. Students will tire of this process, and classroom management is sure to become an issue. If stations are not used in a meaningful way, then this is a waste of learning time. Each learning station should be something that students can do independent of a teacher's support.

Spiraled review concepts should be the topic of many of your stations. These should be based on big ideas and data. I define *spiraled review* as math concepts that have already been taught. There never seems to be enough time to explore number sense and computation. Therefore, many learning station options are grounded in these strands. Data from assessments provides ideas for learning stations, as well. When you monitor and observe students, note their areas of strength and areas where they may need support. When several students need more time to process a concept, put a learning station in place that allows students to practice it.

. . . .

Think Aloud of a Second-Grade Teacher

To give you an idea about how I think through deciding on what topics should be in stations, I've included this "think aloud" as an example.

I'm planning for an upcoming unit on addition and subtraction within 100, and I know that students are expected to fluently add and subtract within 20 using mental strategies. However, many of my students still struggle with this.

I'm going to include learning stations that involve addition and subtraction within 20. After all, I have many students who are not yet fluent with this. I also know that as we move into understanding 100, I will want to add a place value station, since my students have only worked with ones and tens thus far. In addition, in looking ahead, I know that we are going to be moving into our unit on money next. So, I'm going to put a station in that focuses on skip counting and a station on sorting and counting smaller sets of money so that students are ready for that unit when it comes. After all, they probably haven't done anything with this concept since last year.

As a teacher, I look back at what students have done and where they still need more time to develop and solidify those skills. In addition, I look ahead and consider what might support them in being successful.

There are a variety of places to look for resources for learning stations. When I first started math workshop, I stuck with learning station activities that were easy for me—specifically, *Matching* games, *Bingo*, and *Tic-Tac-Toe*. The longer I do math workshop, the more I think about how to make something into a learning station rather than a whole-group lesson. It is amazing what can be done with dice and a set of playing cards. Simple digit cards—whether printed and laminated or hand drawn on construction paper—can make for exciting stations. Sometimes I take a boring worksheet and transform the problems on it into a fun learning station. With a little imagination, you'll find you have the materials and resources necessary to create many learning stations.

Some of My Favorite Books for Learning Stations Ideas

- *Math Games for Number and Operations and Algebraic Thinking: Games to Support Independent Practice in Math Workshops and More, Grades K–5* by Jamee Petersen
- *About Teaching Mathematics, Fourth Edition* by Marilyn Burns
- *How to Differentiate Your Math Instruction* by Linda Dacey, Jayne Bamford Lynch, and Rebeka Eston Salemi
- *It Makes Sense!* series by Melissa Conklin and Stephanie Sheffield
- *Math Work Stations: Extending Learning You Can Count On, K–2* by Debbie Diller

Be intentional about which learning stations to offer and how those options are communicated to students. Math menu organizational systems are especially great for learning station communication. You'll find examples of these and more in the last section of this chapter.

VIDEO CLIP 7.3 ·

Ms. Wallace's Learning Stations

In this clip, Ms. Wallace shares with her first graders the learning stations for the day's math workshop. As you watch this clip, consider the following questions:

- What math concepts are the learning stations targeting?
- How are students provided choice during the learning stations?

To view this video clip, scan the QR code or access via mathsolutions.com/mathworkshop73

· ·

Step 3: Create Learning Station Groups

Depending on the grade level of students and your experience with math workshop, you may allow students to choose with whom they are working during learning stations. However, you may prefer to help students with this choice in the beginning. Consider creating "thinking pairs" or cooperative groups ahead of time. To do this, collect social and formative data on students and thoughtfully use this data in determining learning station groups. Create heterogeneous groups of students for learning stations as opposed to readiness groups (see page 188 in Chapter 8 for more on these types of groups). When students are grouped by readiness for learning stations, teachers often experience classroom management concerns. Placing four struggling students together in one group to work on all learning stations is a recipe for frustration—for students and for the teacher.

Step 4: Determine the System in Which Students Choose Their Learning Stations

Students love to have choices—and learning stations are a great place to give students options. In fact, "children often need to have power over something with a stake and a say in what is happening" (Van de Walle, Karp, and

Bay-Williams 2010, 107). However, when faced with options, students need a system in place that will help them navigate those options—and efficiently make choices. As the teacher, you need to select a system that will communicate to students the activities available, as well as have systems for the presentation and storage of learning stations.

You can be as creative as you like with your organizational system. A popular system is math menus. Types of menus include Must Do/Can Do and Think-Tac-Toe. These menus and more show students options while also encouraging a certain order in how they complete the learning stations; see the final section of this chapter for a more in-depth explanation of each.

Choosing the system that works best for your students and you may be a matter of trial and error. The Pocket Chart math menu, for example, prevents all of my little kindergartners from rushing over to the sorting station that they all love. The Must Do/Can Do math menu encourages students to first complete activities I feel are most critical in supporting the math skills I believe take priority. Each system has its strengths; it really is a matter of finding the one that matches your teaching style and the needs of your unique classroom. If you find that one of the organizational systems you are using doesn't seem to be working for your class, feel free to change it. You may even choose to change it if you feel your students need a fresh way of choosing their learning stations.

Step 5: Determine How Students Move Through the Learning Stations

I've found that there are two ways to move students through learning stations:

1. timed rotations, and
2. open station choice.

Let's look at some of the pros and cons of each.

Timed Rotations In timed rotations, students move to the next learning station after a period of time such as ten minutes. If you choose to use this system, set a timer that goes off to let students know when they need to clean up and move on to another station. In a timed rotation, the same groups of students move from one station to the next. There are advantages and disadvantages to timed rotations (see Figure 7–1).

TIMED ROTATIONS	
PROS	CONS
• As the teacher you are in control of the movement in the classroom; if you see a student moving around before the timer goes off, you know they are not on task. • Students are exposed to all the learning stations. • Ideal for when you have a number of activities that all take a short (and equal) amount of time to complete.	• For timed rotations to succeed, learning stations need to take about the same amount of time to complete (hence the planning and selecting of stations can require a lot more work). • Though I don't recommend it, if you do choose to group students by readiness level, they will often have similar problems with the stations and have no one to help move their thinking.

Figure 7–1. The pros and cons of timed rotations

When I first started math workshop, I used timed rotations. However, I found it challenging and time-consuming to create stations that would all last about the same amount of time. I also found that I was not able to use some activities even though they were really good because of the time that they would take—whether too long or not long enough. I became frustrated with the need to keep each guided math group for the same amount of time. Inevitably, one group would need more time than another.

Students shared my frustration. They would be actively engaged in a station and then the timer would go off. Though they were close to finishing an activity, they had to pack it up and move on. Having to start all over the next day was often met with resistance. Students started to avoid stations they knew took longer, even though the station itself might have been a really good learning activity. If you can relate to this, the second option, open station choice, might work best for you and your students.

Open Station Choice In open station choice, students are in heterogeneous pairs or groups that are determined either by the teacher or by the students themselves (for more on forming groups, see Chapter 8). They choose which stations to go to and for how long they stay. When they complete the station, they put their materials away and make another selection. The teacher calls students to work in guided math groups and keeps them for as long as needed. Learning stations and guided math groups are not confined by a certain amount of time. There are advantages and disadvantages to open station choice (see Figure 7–2 on the next page).

OPEN STATION CHOICE	
PROS	**CONS**
• Students work on the learning station activity for as long as they need (which likely differs for each student). • Students don't have to stop before they're done because a timer goes off, indicating they must rotate to another station.	• Students may choose to stay for the entire time at a learning station they enjoy and miss out on experiencing other stations. • Movement could be happening (and hence be disruptive to other students) during the entire learning station time, not just during timed transitions.

Figure 7–2. The pros and cons of open station choice

What Should I Keep In Mind During Learning Stations?

Once you are fully implementing math workshop you will most likely be meeting with guided math groups as your remaining students move through learning stations. By carefully positioning yourself in guided math groups so that you can have your eyes on all students, you will always have an idea of what's going on during learning stations. It's wonderful to think that every single student is making good choices, working well with others, choosing activities that challenge him or her, persevering through difficult learning stations, and transitioning to the next activity quickly and without disturbing others. However, especially at the beginning, you may find it helpful to do a quick loop of the classroom in between your guided math groups. When monitoring students in learning stations, look for two things especially:

- learning station choice, participation, and behavior; and
- transition time.

Learning Station Choice, Participation, and Behavior

When monitoring students in learning stations, ask yourself, are students:

- staying at a station for what may seem to be too long?
- moving around a bit too much and not spending enough time at any one station to give it their best effort?
- off task?
- avoiding a particular station?
- taking too long to make a choice and/or extending their transition time?
- doing subpar work?

If students are exhibiting any of these behaviors during a learning station, it may be an indication that the station is too difficult, too easy, or too boring (and they just want to get it over with; hence, subpar work). Or maybe the directions are confusing. It could also be an indicator that this is not a good partner match. Make a note to reflect on this station. Ask yourself, "Has this station been around for a while?" If it has, give it a rest. You can bring it out again in the future and see if there is renewed student interest.

What is important to remember is that when you see these behaviors, refer back to the anchor chart and agreements that you made (see the mini-lessons in Chapter 2). What is even more important is that you not let these kinds of behavior scare you off from math workshop.

On the brighter side, don't forget to take note if a station is extremely popular. What makes it so? Note to cycle popular stations back into the mix in upcoming units. Consider inviting a fellow teacher, a mathematics specialist, or an administrator in to the classroom to take notes and report on what is going on in the stations. Sometimes it is really nice to have a third party see things that you don't while you are working with your guided math group.

When in doubt, ask students to tell you or write about the stations. Give them writing prompts such as, *What is your favorite learning station? Why? What is your least favorite learning station? Why?* Don't be afraid to pull a station after the first day if it is appearing to not be a good choice. One thing you can be sure of: your stations will get better and better throughout the year. The more you monitor learning stations, the more you will see what your students need and what kinds of ways they prefer to learn.

Transition Time

How long is it taking students to move from one station to another? Transition time is time off task. When monitoring students as they move through learning stations, be on the lookout for the student who takes an extreme amount of time walking from one station to another or too much time choosing the next station. Also consider how long it takes for students to get started in a learning station. I was once in a fourth-grade classroom that had a technology station. Great idea, right? Well, once students arrived at the computers, it took them at least ten minutes to log on and type in the URL. This ten minutes is not learning time. When time is being wasted on getting started, consider how you might streamline the station's process so that students can more quickly get to the mathematics. A quick tweak, ensuring the website was pulled up in advance, helped make the technology station a success!

But, I have one student who just can't handle learning stations! What do I do?

I get it—this can be a difficult dilemma. My guess is that this one student is also someone who you have to plan differently for in reading and writing workshop, the cafeteria, and more. This may be the kid whose agenda you have to check each day, whose desk you have to clean out once a week to find their missing work, and who needs at least three copies of the field trip permission form.

The key is to make sure you don't plan your entire class around this student. If you let this one student be the reason that math workshop does not happen in your classroom, you are letting this one student hold you back from providing the best instruction for all your students. Instead, here are some suggestions for how to support this student:

- Put a star next to the learning station that you want this student to work on first. Ask the student to check in with you before they move to another station.
- Have a special folder for this student to keep any unfinished work.
- Determine the partner for this student ahead of time. Remember to switch this often.
- Position the student's work space near you when she is completing learning stations.
- Provide this student with a different math menu that is on the same colored paper as the other students. This may have fewer stations or stations numbered in the order that the student should complete the activities.

 **VIDEO CLIP 7.4**

Transitioning to Learning Stations

In this clip, Ms. Robinson transitions her class of second graders to their learning stations during math workshop. As you watch this clip, consider the following question:

- What do you notice about the routines and procedures that Ms. Robinson has put in place?

To view this video clip, scan the QR code or access via mathsolutions.com/mathworkshop74

What Should I Keep in Mind About Accountability in Learning Stations?

So, what do you do to ensure students are accountable for their work during learning stations? First, don't feel that you need to have paper and pencils at every station. In fact, you shouldn't. Station activities are meant to be engaging and purposeful. This can include problem solving, partner games, time on the computer, and time to explore. If I have a station for kindergartners to work on sorting, I don't need them to complete a worksheet to evaluate this. Rather, I should walk over to them and ask them how they are sorting. The teacher that puts a worksheet at each station in order to hold students accountable for their work is bound to give up on math workshop after they spend their entire weekend grading the enormous stack of papers that they had to take home. Don't do that to yourself. And, more importantly, don't do that to your students. Instead, offer appropriate and exciting stations to keep students engaged. Students will *want* to complete these stations and will even look forward to this time in math workshop.

What Do Learning Stations Look Like During Math Workshop?

The organizational system you use to communicate station options to your students will drive how your math workshop looks during learning stations. One of my favorite systems is math menus. Math menus are most frequently presented in the form of a choice board. Depending on the type of math menu you choose, you might provide each student with their own paper copy, or you could have one displayed for the entire class on chart paper or a whiteboard. In this section I briefly share some of my favorite math menus.

My Favorite Math Menus for Math Workshop

- Dining Out
- List It
- Must Do/Can Do
- Think–Tac–Toe
- Pocket Charts

Math Menu: Dining Out

This type of math menu literally uses a menu structure to feature activities focused on certain mathematical topics. For example, number sense activities may be available as appetizers. Spiraled activities (as deemed by data) may be the main entrees, and activities that correspond with the current unit of study might be dessert choices. I encourage students to write about their thinking as they move from station to station, jotting down questions they might have or observations that they are making during the activities. These notes can be especially helpful when students return to a station for a second time. (See Figure 7–1; Reproducible 7 offers a template for Dining Out menus.)

See Reproducible 7 for a template to create your own Dining Out menu.

Math Menu: Dining Out Template

	Write about it:
Appetizers (choose 2) ❏ Cooking Up Math ❏ Number Tiles ❏ Sizzling Problems ❏ Fraction War	
Entrée (choose 1) ❏ Order Some Decimals ❏ Decimal Puzzle ❏ Decimal Dash	Write about it:
Side Dish (choose 2) ❏ Multiplication Mania ❏ Multiple Madness ❏ Division Matching	Write about it:
Dessert (choose 1) ❏ Measurement Olympics ❏ Moving with Measurement ❏ Measure Me	Write about it:

Figure 7–3. Math Menu: Dining Out sample

 **VIDEO CLIP 7.5** ·

Math Menu: Dining Out

In this clip, Ms. Callaway transitions her fifth graders to their learning stations using a Dining Out math menu. We then see partners working together and reflecting on their learning stations. As you watch this clip, consider the following questions:

- Think about the three buckets of math workshop (classroom arrangement, routines and procedures, and mathematics community), first introduced in Chapter 2. What do you notice with Ms. Callaway's class that indicates these buckets are "full" and hence an effective and successful math workshop can transpire?

- What stands out to you about how the students work together as well as reflect on their learning stations?

To view this video clip, scan the QR code or access via mathsolutions.com/mathworkshop75

· ·

Math Menu: List It

List It math menus are often used at the primary level and found most often in kindergarten. In a List It menu the name of the stations or pictures of the stations are placed in each of the boxes or blanks. There is also a reflection piece built in at the end. You might choose to tape each student's list to their desk; students are then responsible for coloring in the box once they have been to the station. There are often "rules" for the list, such as a student may not revisit a station until they have participated in each one. (See Figure 7–4; Reproducible 8 offers a template for List It.)

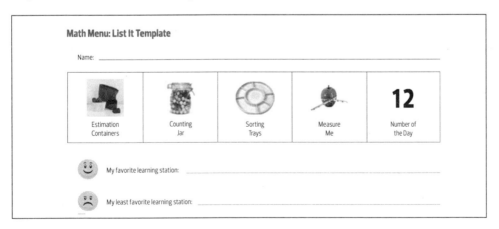

> See Reproducible 8 for a template to create your own List It menu.

Figure 7–4. Math Menu: List It sample

Math Menu: Must Do/Can Do

A Must Do/Can Do math menu communicates some activities as nonnegotiable (the Must Dos) and others as options after the Must Dos are completed (the Can Dos). Choosing the order of the Must Dos as well as which of the Can Do activities to complete provides students with some control of their learning. A reflection component at the end helps students think deeply about their learning. (See Figure 7–5; Reproducible 9 offers a template for Must Do/Can Do.)

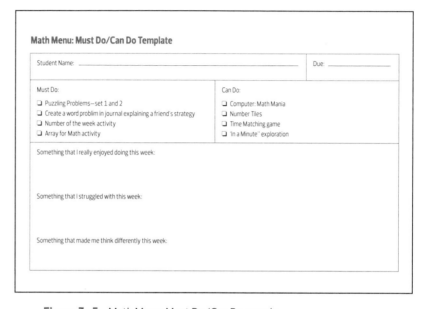

Figure 7–5. Math Menu: Must Do/Can Do sample

See Reproducible 9 for a template to create your own Must Do/ Can Do menu.

· ·

Using an Interactive Whiteboard for Must Do/Can Do

Ms. McGonigal uses an interactive whiteboard to post a Must Do/Can Do math menu for her third graders. She explains her organizational system as follows:

"To organize my learning stations, I use a Must Do/Can Do with my SMART Board. I have a set list of activities that students can choose from, and under each activity I have six boxes.

Students know that only six students can work in each activity at a time. I have a picture of each student off to the side of the SMART Board, and students have the choice of where they want to go. They'll drag their picture to that station as long as there's an empty box. This way they know which activity they're doing, they know who else is doing that station, and they know who they can work with. And then, I have a set area in my classroom where all the materials for the activities are kept, and they're labeled, corresponding to the SMART Board. Students know to go there to get what they need. Materials are usually organized in sandwich bags. I like to have about four or five sets of the same game, all in sandwich bags in a box. So, when students come over, they just take a bag out of the box for the activity they're doing. If there's a recording sheet that goes along with the activity, I keep it in an envelope in that same box and students know to just pull that out as well and take it with them."

 VIDEO CLIP 7.6

Math Menu: Must Do/Can Do

In this clip, we see excerpts of Ms. Hrabak facilitating a math workshop with her fourth graders using a Must Do/Can Do menu. She also shares insights on what she does to ensure a successful math workshop. As you watch this clip, consider the following questions:

- What do you notice about the routines and procedures that Ms. Hrabak has put in place?
- What are some of the ways Ms. Hrabak holds her students accountable in learning stations?

To see the rest of Ms. Hrabak's math workshop, refer to Video Clip 4.1.

To view this video clip, scan the QR code or access via mathsolutions.com/mathworkshop76

Math Menu: Think–Tac–Toe

A Think-Tac-Toe math menu can be especially useful for differentiation; it may include learning stations that differ by readiness, interest, and learning profile. For example, all the activities in the first row might address number sense and computation. The second row might have activities around the current unit of study, and the third row could be about topics that you have seen students struggle with in class. The rows could be differentiated by level of rigor.

You might require that students complete one activity from each column, do the middle activity first, or even challenge them to "clear the board." (See Figure 7–6; Reproducible 10 offers a template for a Think-Tac-Toe math menu.)

> For a video of Think-Tac-Toe in action, see Video Clip 7.3 in the resource *How to Differentiate Your Math Instruction* (Dacey, Bamford Lynch, Eston Salemi 2013).

Math Menu: Think-Tac-Toe Template

Multiplication War Cards	Puzzling Problems	Division Dominoes
Number Tiles	Place Your Order	Puzzling Problem
Chip Away	Puzzling Problem	Computer: x-madness

My favorite activity this week was _____

because _____

_____

_____ .

The most challenging activity this week was _____

because _____

_____

_____ .

See Reproducible 10 for a template to create your own Think-Tac-Toe menu.

Figure 7–6. Math Menu: Think–Tac–Toe sample

Math Menu: Pocket Charts

A Pocket Chart math menu is often used in primary grades, however it is also successful with upper elementary classes. Place cards with the names or pictures of the learning station options on the far left side of a pocket chart. Then make a card for each student, showing the student's picture and name. Consider placing students at the learning station you want them to do first. Once they have completed that activity, they can choose another station and move their cards next to that activity. I have found that helping very young students with determining their first learning station prevents a large group of students from all rushing to one favorite station.

Figure 7–7. Math Menu: Pocket Chart sample

VIDEO CLIP 7.7

Math Menu: Pocket Chart

In this clip, Ms. Griswold uses a pocket chart during math workshop with her kindergarteners. As you watch this clip, consider the following questions:

• Think about the three buckets of math workshop (classroom arrangement, routines and procedures, and mathematics community), first introduced in Chapter 2. What do you notice with Ms. Griswold's class that indicates these buckets are "full" and hence an effective and successful math workshop can transpire?

• Near the end of this clip we see Ms. Griswold join a group of students at the Pattern Blocks station. What do you notice about Ms. Griswold's role during this time?

To view this video clip, scan the QR code or access via mathsolutions.com/mathworkshop77

Connecting the Chapter to Your Practice

- Think about the activities that you do with your students. Which ones might you consider making into learning stations? What would you need to do for this to happen?

- What are some math concepts that your students typically need more time to process? With those concepts in mind, what activities could you add to learning stations that would allow students to practice these concepts in an accessible and engaging way?

- What are the "big ideas" at your grade level? How might you consider these when choosing or creating learning stations?

- What types of math menus might you use to communicate learning station options to your students?

- If you have already been using learning stations in your classroom, ask yourself these questions:
  - Are my learning stations going well? Why or why not? What could I do to improve them?

- How have I set up expectations for students to work in learning stations?
- How have I helped students practice transitioning from one learning station to another?
- How do students know who they can work with?
- Which stations do I want to keep again for another time in the year? Which stations might I want to get rid of now?

 VIDEO CLIPS 4.1 and 5.1, Revisited ·

Rewatch these two clips; this time pay special attention to the learning stations section of each clip and consider the following questions:

- What do you see happening in the learning stations?
- How does the learning station component of each math workshop structure contribute to the overall effectiveness and success of the structure?

Video Clip 4.1   Video Clip 5.1

To view these video clips, scan the QR codes or access via mathsolutions.com/mathworkshop41 and mathsolutions.com/mathworkshop51

Guided Math

Chapter 8

(continued)

VIDEO CLIP 8.1 ·······························

A Guided Math Group: What Is Symmetry?

In this clip, Ms. Robinson guides a small group of second graders through an activity focused on symmetry. As you watch this clip, consider the following questions:

• What do you think is the purpose of this guided math group?

• What makes this small group time valuable?
• What is the role of the teacher? Students?
• What questions do you have about guided math?

To view this video clip, scan the QR code or access via mathsolutions.com/mathworkshop81

· ·

What Is Guided Math?

Guided math is small-group instruction that allows the teacher to support and learn more about students' understandings and misconceptions.

MATH WORKSHOP: TASK AND SHARE		MATH WORKSHOP: FOCUS LESSON, GUIDED MATH, AND LEARNING STATIONS			MATH WORKSHOP: GUIDED MATH AND LEARNING STATIONS		
5–10 minutes	NUMBER SENSE ROUTINE	5–10 minutes	NUMBER SENSE ROUTINE		5–10 minutes	NUMBER SENSE ROUTINE	
30 minutes	MATH TASK	15 minutes	FOCUS LESSON		45 minutes	GUIDED MATH	LEARNING STATIONS
		30 minutes	GUIDED MATH	LEARNING STATIONS			
20–25 minutes	TASK SHARE WITH STUDENT REFLECTION	5–10 minutes	STUDENT REFLECTION		5–10 minutes	STUDENT REFLECTION	

The term *guided math* has taken on a life of its own in education. In several schools, I've heard *guided math* used to describe the entire math class. For the purpose of this book, the term describes small-group instruction time, facilitated by the teacher and occurring during math workshop alongside learning stations. In guided math the teacher intentionally selects students to support and learn more about their understandings and misconceptions. Think of guided math as one component of math workshop, just as guided reading is one component of reading workshop. While small-group instruction is not a novel concept, small-group instruction *in mathematics* may be new to some.

There are two main categories of guided math groups:

1. *Small-group instruction:* This category comprises any group of two or more students intentionally selected by the teacher.

2. *One-on-one conferencing:* This category involves just one student; it is the teacher's time to meet with individual students one-on-one.

Why Have Guided Math?

Fountas and Pinnell (2001) state that focused teaching in small groups makes it possible to provide appropriate instruction. It is through small-group instruction that differentiation can happen; as teachers we can gather a great deal of information on each student. It can be overwhelmingly difficult when faced with trying to do this during whole-group instruction; we've all looked at our sea of students and seen expressions of confusion, distraction, and even boredom (especially when there are students who already know the information being presented). When we work with students in small groups, providing the instruction they need when they need it, we are better able to address individual needs, keep students engaged, understand their strengths and struggles, and ultimately foster a growth mindset, building not only students' mathematics knowledge but also their confidence.

Reflect on It!

What excites you most about working with small groups of students in math class?

When Should I Use Guided Math?

Guided math groups are found in two of the three math workshop structures: Focus Lesson, Guided Math, and Learning Stations (see Chapter 4) and Guided Math and Learning Stations (see Chapter 5). When you've chosen to do one of these two structures, I recommend you follow three steps to making guided math part of your math workshop:

1. Establish math workshop routines and procedures.
2. Pull just one guided math group.
3. Pull more than one guided math group.

Step 1: Establish Math Workshop Routines and Procedures

Why not jump right into using guided math groups? With this component of math workshop it's especially critical that you *Go Slow to Go Fast*. I understand the temptation to pull a small group immediately. However, by pulling small groups too early, you might not have established the routines and procedures that will keep the rest of your math workshop—those students not in your guided math group—engaged and working cooperatively. You could end up with a classroom management nightmare. A clear plan for students who are not in guided math must be in place to successfully implement guided math within math workshop. Completing the twenty minilessons (see Chapter 2) with students is a great way to kick-start student expectations and understandings for what to do when they are not part of a guided math group. Completing these lessons will also give you confidence that students are making good choices while working apart from you.

Consider using the three buckets (first introduced in Chapter 2) as your checklist to determining if your students and you are ready for guided math:

 Classroom Arrangement

Look around your room. Is your space arranged to be as conducive as possible to math workshop?

 Routines and Procedures

Have you spent time practicing learning stations and transitions with students?

See Chapter 2 to review the twenty minilessons and the three buckets.

 Mathematics Community

Are your students talking with one another, explaining their thinking, working together, respecting each other's ideas, and exhibiting a growth mindset?

If you've answered "yes" to these three questions, then you and your students are likely ready for the next step!

Step 2: Pull Just One Guided Math Group

Once you establish your routines and procedures, and you are ready to pull a small group of students, I recommend that you stick to just one guided math group on the first day. This gives you time to monitor students in learning stations as well.

To do this, first announce to students that you plan to work with a guided math group. Keep your guided math group lesson under fifteen minutes. Following the lesson, monitor students in learning stations and provide feedback. If during your guided math lesson you notice students exhibiting unacceptable behaviors at the stations, do a quick "catch and release." Stand up, get the attention of all students, and explain to them that their behavior is prohibiting you from being able to work with a small group. If needed, revisit with the whole class one of the minilessons in Chapter 2 that discuss appropriate behavior.

Step 3: Pull More Than One Guided Math Group

Each day, assuming student behavior allows it, decrease the amount of time spent monitoring stations after your guided math group. This will allow you to start pulling more guided math groups. Figure 8–1 shows the progression to more and more guided math groups:

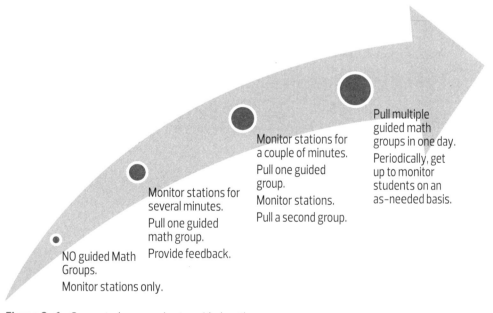

Pull multiple guided math groups in one day. Periodically, get up to monitor students on an as-needed basis.

Monitor stations for a couple of minutes.
Pull one guided group.
Monitor stations.
Pull a second group.

Monitor stations for several minutes.
Pull one guided math group.
Provide feedback.

NO guided Math Groups.
Monitor stations only.

Figure 8–1. Suggested progression to guided math groups

How many guided math groups should you ultimately be meeting with each day? That depends! This is just one of the wonderful characteristics of math workshop; it is flexible, unlike the traditional model of instruction. Math workshop allows you to make each day exactly what you want it to be. Some days you may meet with one guided math group, while other days you might meet with four.

Regardless of how many guided math groups you hold in a day, it is important to limit each group's time to no more than fifteen minutes. This can be challenging; even now, after doing guided math groups for years, I use a timer for myself to ensure that I do not spend too much time with any one group. I also try to keep in mind that if I'm feeling like a group needs more than fifteen minutes, I may be trying to tackle too much in one meeting. Students need time to process.

When meeting with a struggling group of students, as teachers we can feel tempted to think that if we just keep them for a few more minutes, all will become clear to them. However, in doing this, we may only ever meet with our struggling students. This is not fair for two important reasons:

1. Struggling students need time to explore the learning stations, too. Learning stations are not just for students who are doing well in class.

2. Students who are not struggling—and those who are performing above grade level—need small-group instruction, too; we want all students to make a year's worth of growth!

The key thing to remember is that *fair isn't always equal*. Don't keep a group for fifteen minutes just because you kept the last group for fifteen minutes. You do not need to pull each guided group for the same amount of time. Be intentional about what you are doing with them.

> The key thing to remember is that *fair isn't always equal*. Don't keep a group for fifteen minutes just because you kept the last group for fifteen minutes. You do not need to pull each guided group for the same amount of time.

Reflect on It!

How do you meet the individual needs of students in your current math class structure?

Help! I feel guilty! I'm not meeting with every student every day!

Does this statement resonate with you during math workshop? If so, don't feel guilty! You *are* meeting with everyone each day. By choosing math workshop as your model of instruction, you are holding an engaging and rich number sense routine as a warm-up. You are ending the lesson with a powerful reflection. You are monitoring students within learning stations. Just because you didn't get to pull each student for a guided math group each day doesn't mean that they haven't been deeply engrossed in mathematical thinking. The learning stations that students are experiencing and the mathematical community that has been established allows for students to learn from someone other than just you, the teacher. Isn't that what we want? So, throw away that guilt and get back to planning for those students.

What Should I Keep in Mind When Forming Guided Math Groups?

You might be wondering *how* to decide on the groups of students to work with in guided math; this question was first addressed in Chapter 5. I suggest three ways to group students for guided math lessons:

1. Readiness grouping
2. Heterogeneous grouping
3. Random grouping

See Chapter 5 for more on choosing groups for guided math.

It is important that as teachers we use all three of these groupings on a continual basis. Imagine a classroom where the teacher only uses readiness groups; students might quickly notice that they are always with a group of students that excel or with a group of students that have been struggling. This can harm both the mathematical community and the mindset of the students. Let's take a closer look at each of the three groupings.

Readiness Grouping

Readiness grouping is perhaps the most familiar way to place students in a guided math group. In this type of group, the teacher works with students who have a similar strength or need. These groups are based on data that shows students' strengths and weaknesses. As teachers we may typically use an exit ticket or pretest data to create these groups. We might also use data gathered from our observations or other formative assessments. For example, I noticed that five students were struggling with using the ruler to measure length to the half-inch. I decided to pull these five students into a guided math group and work with them to gain mastery of this new skill.

Heterogeneous Grouping

Heterogeneous grouping combines students with various strengths, struggles, learning styles, strategy preferences, and interests. It is especially great for problem solving. When we have a heterogeneous group of students working to solve problems, we are more likely to get a variety of strategies and have a rich, powerful, strategy-sharing discussion. From the student who struggles most to the most advanced student, everyone can benefit from this form of grouping.

Random Grouping

Random grouping is great for data collection. The teacher may call a random group of students in order to work with them as a means to collect information. This could be something as simple as a teacher asking all the students from the "blue" table to come back. They are given a set of number cards to order from least to greatest. The teacher watches this, takes notes about the students' performance, and uses this data later to help drive instruction like lessons to choose or decisions about future groups.

Reflect on It!

How do you group your students? Why do you group them that way?

What Should I Keep in Mind When Doing One-on-One Conferencing?

As mentioned at the beginning of this chapter, one-on-one conferencing is considered a category of guided math groups. Just as in writing workshop, where the teacher meets with one student to discuss their writing piece, there are times in math workshop when it is appropriate to meet with just one student to discuss their mathematical thinking. This conferencing is done on an "as-needed" basis and can take anywhere from one to ten minutes. Sometimes I just need to ask clarifying questions about a student's work so that I can be clearer about their understanding. Sometimes I need to sit down with one student and assess what he or she knows. And sometimes I may notice that a student is showing evidence of an error pattern that I believe can be easily corrected with a few one-on-one minutes.

This is also the time to conduct individual interviews with students. Do you need to find out if a student can count forward to one hundred? It is best to just call the student over and ask them to count for you, right? A great resource for learning more about individual interviews is *How to Assess While You Teach Math, Grades K–2* by Dana Islas (2011). It includes videos of student conferences in action. A resource appropriate for upper elementary is Marilyn Burns's Math Reasoning Inventory (*www.mathreasoninginventory.com*), which also includes videos of actual interviews.

What Does a Guided Math Group Look Like During Math Workshop?

Think back to the rules of thumb established about whole-group focus lessons in Chapter 4, page 123. These rules also apply to guided math groups. In a nutshell, a strong guided math group should have the following happening in it:

- students are being encouraged to show their strategies;
- time is being allowed for exploration; and
- there is use of student talk and talk moves.

 **VIDEO CLIP 8.2** ·

A Guided Math Group: Problem Solving

In this clip, Ms. McGonigal guides a small group of third graders through a problem-solving task. As you watch this clip, consider the following questions:

- Ms. McGonigal chose not to reveal the numbers in the word problem right away. Why do you think she chose to do this? What would be the benefits of presenting a math problem in this way?
- What do you notice about the process Ms. McGonigal takes her group through to solve the problem? How is this process similar to or different from the way you facilitate problem solving with your students?
- What do you notice about when and how Ms. McGonigal is taking notes?

To view this video clip, scan the QR code or access via mathsolutions.com/mathworkshop82

· ·

So what might you do during a guided math lesson? Anything that you would do during a whole-group focus lesson is appropriate for guided math. The difference is that you will have the attention of fewer students, so you will be able to analyze their thinking more closely and respond immediately to what you see and hear. I've found the following to be great for guided math groups:

- facilitating a focus lesson
- problem solving
- reinforcing a new learning station

- assessing students
- discussing common errors
- providing intervention

Let's look at each one of these more in depth.

Facilitating a Focus Lesson

If you are using the Guided Math and Learning Stations structure (see Chapter 5), then the focus lesson is introduced during guided math time. This allows you to have a greater impact on individual students than when you do a whole-group focus lesson, especially if you find that not everyone in the class is in need of the lesson. When a focus lesson is done with fewer students, we can more clearly identify the strategies that students use, the solidity of their understandings, and the misconceptions that surface.

Problem Solving

Consider using guided math groups to support students in sharing and making connections among strategies. To do this, apply the same practices implemented in the Task and Share structure of math workshop (see Chapter 3), only in a small-group context. See page 112 in Chapter 3 for these five practices (anticipate, monitor, select, sequence, connect).

Reinforcing a New Learning Station

The Focus Lesson, Guided Math, and Learning Stations structure (see Chapter 4) is a great way to introduce new learning stations to students. However, if some students need more time with the learning station before working at it on their own, consider pulling them into a guided math group focused on reinforcing the station. I get a lot of information during this time, and will even make the decision to scrap the station all together if students are finding the station to be too difficult, too easy, or boring.

Assessing Students

One of the many attributes of guided math time is that it helps you as the teacher gain a clearer picture of students' understanding and misunderstandings. There are many topics in mathematics that are more easily assessed in a small-group or interview-style format rather than by paper and pencil. By assessing during a guided math lesson, as teachers we can use the data collected to help plan for upcoming lessons and determine groups of students with like needs.

Discussing Common Errors

Guided math can be a valuable time to help students analyze their own misconceptions and avoid those error patterns in the future. When a student's misconception is not clear, pull them aside for one-on-one conferencing to gain clarity. You may also work with a small group of students who all share the same misconceptions as evidenced by work samples, classroom discussions, or assessments.

Providing Intervention

Guided math can also be a valuable time to help you fill in the gaps that you notice in student understanding. As teachers we have all had students come to us who are not yet ready for some of the grade-level curriculum. By working with these students in guided math groups, we can support them with the content they need most.

What do I write down about my students in guided math groups?

To answer this question, ask yourself: what do you write down for reading workshop? Typically, teachers jot down notes about what they see students doing, what strengths students may exhibit, what students might be struggling with, and what strategies students use. It is the same for math.

What strengths or struggles do I see?
For example, I might see that a student easily uses benchmark fractions as a means to compare a list of fractions and I'll note this as a strength. I might also see that the student is having difficulty determining a common numerator or denominator when comparing a list of fractions. I'll note that as a struggle.

What strategies are being used?
In observing students as they solve 4 + 7, I may note that Tara builds using counters and counts all. Hailey counts up from four and Miguel counts up from 7. Leo attempts to use his fingers, but gets stuck building both numbers.

Keep in mind that these notes will help you make instructional decisions later. Write down everything you think may help you to determine groups, lessons, feedback to students, communication with parents, and reporting grades. I let students know that I will write down things during our time together so they don't worry why I'm writing. I usually joke that my mind can't remember all the wonderful things they do, so I have to write them down.

As part of guided math groups, it's important to figure out a system that's easy to maintain in noting and remembering students' thinking. Groups in math workshop are often much more fluid than groups in reading workshop. I have found that keeping my note pages simple has worked out best. I use blank checklists and tables to jot down my observations. I also never keep my records on sticky notes. They always seem to get lost, or I find random sticky notes on the bottom of my shoe at the end of the day! I include three of my favorite anecdotal records templates in this resource; see Reproducibles 11, 12, and 13. See Figures 8–2, 8–3, and 8–4 on the following pages for examples of how I might fill these templates. Bottom line: Do what works best for you.

> **See Reproducibles 11, 12, and 13 for anecdotal records templates.**

MATH PROBLEM	STUDENT NAME AND STRATEGIES/OBSERVATIONS			
Sarah biked 9 miles and June biked 7 miles. How many miles did the two girls bike?	Garrett Used doubles: 7 + 7 = 14 14 + 2 = 16	Rochelle Knew that 10 + 7 = 17. One less is 16.	Amberleigh Took one from the 7 and gave it to the 9 to make it a 10. Then 10 + 6 = 16	Mikey Same as Rochelle: 10 + 7 = 17 17 – 1 = 16
On day 1, Mike read 27 pages of this book. On day 2, he read 25 pages. How many pages did Mike read in those two days?	SarahBeth 27 + 20 = 47 47 (fingers up) 48, 49, 50, 51, 52	Andre knew 25 + 25 = 50 (referred to quarters) 50 + 2 = 52	Martina Tens and ones 20 + 20 = 40 7 + 5 = 12 40 + 12 = 52	Luca Tens and ones 20 + 20 = 40 7 + 5 = 13 * 40 + 10 = 50 50 + 3 = 53 *check back about error

Figure 8–2. Anecdotal records for recording student strategies and observations (see Reproducible 11)

STUDENT NAME	COUNTS FORWARD 1–10	COUNTS FORWARD 1–30	COUNTS FORWARD 1–50	COUNTS FORWARD 1–100	COUNTS BACKWARD 30–0	SKIP-COUNTS BY 10 TO 100	SKIP-COUNTS BY 5 TO 100
Jose	9/15	10/1	12/1	12/1		12/12	
Amelia	9/15	9/15	12/1				
Omar	9/15	9/15	12/1				
Celina	9/16	10/9					
Rachelle	9/15	9/15	9/15	9/15			
Ilene	9/16	9/16					
Frankie	9/16	9/16	9/16	9/16			

Figure 8–3. Anecdotal records for tracking date of mastery (see Reproducible 12)

INSTRUCTIONAL GOAL: _students will compare fractions_				
STUDENT NAME	ANTICIPATED MATH STRATEGY			
	USED BENCHMARK FRACTIONS	FOUND COMMON DENOMINATOR	FOUND COMMON NUMERATOR	COOKIES AND KIDS
Sheliah			✓	
Connor				✓
Mitchel	✓			
Gavin	✓			

Figure 8–4. Anecdotal records for tracking anticipated strategies (see Reproducible 13)

Connecting the Chapter to Your Practice

- Think about how your students are currently exploring topics in math class. What information do you have that would help you form guided math groups?

- Do you use small-group instruction in any other subject area? What benefits do you see when you instruct in small groups? What do you find challenging?

- How might the twenty minilessons (see Chapter 2) help ensure that students are engaged in learning stations so that you are more able to pull students into guided math groups?

- If you are already using guided math in your classroom, ask yourself the following:

  - Do I use data to support the readiness groups that I meet with during guided math time? If so, do I believe that the data points that I use provide an accurate picture of each student's strengths and struggles? If not, what other data might I need to help me determine my course of action?

  - Do I change up my guided math groups so that the same students don't always work together? Do students in my class work with varied groups of students, or do they tend to work with the same students over and over again? If the latter, what can I do to change this?

- When it is time to form new guided math groups, what data will I use to decide those groups?

VIDEO CLIPS 4.1 and 5.1, Revisited ·

Rewatch these two clips, paying special attention to the guided math part of each video and consider the following questions:

- What is the purpose of each guided math group?
- What makes this small group time valuable?
- What is the role of the teacher? Students?

- How does the guided math component of each math workshop structure contribute to the overall effectiveness and success of the structure?

Video Clip 4.1   Video Clip 5.1

To view these video clips, scan the QR codes or access via mathsolutions.com/mathworkshop41 and mathsolutions.com/mathworkshop51

Student Reflection

CHAPTER 9

What Is Student Reflection?

Student reflection is a deliberate and meaningful time for students to consider new learning.

MATH WORKSHOP: TASK AND SHARE		MATH WORKSHOP: FOCUS LESSON, GUIDED MATH, AND LEARNING STATIONS			MATH WORKSHOP: GUIDED MATH AND LEARNING STATIONS		
5–10 minutes	NUMBER SENSE ROUTINE	5–10 minutes	NUMBER SENSE ROUTINE		5–10 minutes	NUMBER SENSE ROUTINE	
30 minutes	MATH TASK	15 minutes	FOCUS LESSON		45 minutes	GUIDED MATH	LEARNING STATIONS
		30 minutes	GUIDED MATH	LEARNING STATIONS			
20–25 minutes	STUDENT REFLECTION	5–10 minutes	STUDENT REFLECTION		5–10 minutes	STUDENT REFLECTION	

Student reflection is the final component of all the math workshop structures. It is a deliberate and meaningful time for students to reflect on what they've learned and experienced during a math task, at activities in learning stations, or in a guided math group. Maggie Siena (2009) refers to the time for students to share strategies and answers as math shares. If we choose to do a math share for student reflection, we make careful choices about whose strategy to share and in what order. By sequencing strategies from least to most sophisticated or concrete to abstract, we help students make connections. We might also choose to share a spectrum of strategies from those most often used by students to those that are not as frequently seen or used. See Chapter 3 (page 112), for five practices to use when choosing and sharing student strategies.

Other forms of student reflection might be to ask students to write to a prompt in their math journal, answer a question with a partner, complete an exit ticket, or share about a moment in the day's learning (see the last section of this chapter for more details on these reflection formats and more).

write in Math journal

Why Use Student Reflection?

There is a lot of research about the benefits of reflection. During reflection, students make mathematical connections. This is where most of the learning happens. Students share strategies, compare strategies, and analyze strategies for effectiveness and efficiency. Students reflect on what was difficult and what came more easily to them. They contemplate their new understandings and consider what they are still grappling with.

make mathematical connections

When Should I Use Student Reflection?

Student reflection transpires in the last five to ten minutes of math workshop. Unfortunately, reflection time is often left out—because time runs out. It's critical that we make time for reflection. Set your watch, cell phone, timer— do whatever you need to do to remind yourself that it's time for reflection. I remember, in my early days of teaching, looking up at the clock and realizing that there were only a few minutes left of class. My "reflection" often got shoved to the back burner and I ended my class abruptly, saying something along the lines of, "So, this is your homework, put your things away, and line up for art—now." I'm saddened to think of the learning opportunities my students missed because I skipped the reflection. It is often during this reflection process that the greatest learning takes place.

What Should I Keep In Mind During Student Reflection?

While your role during reflection time will vary depending on the type of reflection that you have chosen to use, your outcomes during this time will be the same. During reflection, your desired outcomes are the following:

- gather data about students' self-perception of their strengths and weaknesses;
- monitor student progress on the mathematical concept or skill;
- share student thinking/strategies/questions/concerns/considerations; and
- have students understand the mathematics more deeply.

Four Possible Desired Outcomes of Student Reflection

· gather data
· monitor student progress
· provide time for students to share
· encourage students to understand the mathematics more deeply

If you are just getting started, consider one or two of these desired outcomes to focus on first and ask yourself the questions associated with them.

- If your desired outcome is to *gather data* about student's self-perception, how will you make note of that and how will it impact your instruction?

- If your desired outcome is to *monitor student progress* on the mathematical concept or skill, will you sort student work into groups or make some anecdotal records or teaching notes to yourself so you can address needs in a guided math group or extend with a learning station activity?

- If your desired outcome is to *provide time for students to share*, what will you look for—and what do you hope to learn during this sharing about student understanding, perceptions, and effort?

- If your desired outcome is to *encourage students to understand the mathematics more deeply*, what evidence will you look for that you were successful with this? If you were successful, how will this inform your selection of upcoming math lessons? If you weren't successful, what learning stations or guided math groups will you need to incorporate into math workshop to meet students' needs?

What Does a Student Reflection Look Like During Math Workshop?

In this section I share some of my favorite ways to have students reflect on their learning. You are certainly not limited to these ways. However, if finding the time to reflect has been a challenge for you or if you feel stuck with using the same reflection format each day, consider one of these ideas. You might also choose a reflection format that works best with what you're trying to find out. Are you trying to gauge how students perceive the changes to the math block structure? Or are you hoping to dig a little deeper into students' mindsets about mathematics in general or about a specific activity that you are doing in class? Do you need specific data to help you form groups for tomorrow?

Ideas for Student Reflections

- Math Share
- Journal Prompts
- Turn and Talk
- Get Moving
- Exit Tickets
- Four Corners

Math Share

Math share is used as an example of a type of student reflection at the beginning of this chapter. During a math share, students share their thinking and make connections among various strategies. This reflection format can also be used when students have all had a similar Must Do activity to complete. For example, kindergartners may all be working on creating patterns; in a Must Do learning station each student has drawn a representation of their favorite pattern on a sentence strip. To start their math share, students sit in a circle on the carpet with their pattern. Each student takes a turn sharing their pattern with the rest of the class. The teacher asks questions such as:

- *Could someone tell us what pattern _____ [student name] created?*
- *Could someone tell us what would come next in this pattern?*
- *Does anyone have a pattern similar to _____'s pattern?*

Another example may be a group of fourth graders who have been working on the idea of remainders. As part of math workshop, students were put into groups and tasked with solving the following problems:

Group A	Group B	Group C	Group D
There are 33 pieces of candy being put into 4 bags. If I want each bag to have the same amount of candy, how many pieces will go into each bag?	The bike relay race is 33 miles. If there are 4 members on the team, how far will each person have to bike if they are to bike an equal amount?	There are 33 students going on a field trip. We can put 4 students into each car. How many cars will we need?	There are 33 dogs that need to be washed at the doggie spa. There are 4 people working today who will share the job. How many dogs will each person wash?

When it is time for reflection, students gather on the carpet to share. Each group shares their problem with the class and then discusses the ways they went about solving it. The teacher asks questions such as:

- *In all four of these problems, we see the numbers 33 and 4. Why are your answers different?*

- *What did your group need to consider when solving your problem?*

- *How did the problem-solving strategy you used support your decision making?*

 VIDEO CLIP 9.1

Student Reflection: Math Share

In this clip, Ms. Griswold brings kindergartners together for a math share as the student reflection part of math workshop. As you watch this clip, consider the following questions:

- What do you notice about this reflection?
- Think about the possible desired outcomes of reflection (listed on page 200 in this chapter). What do you think Ms. Griswold's desired outcomes were for this reflection?

To view this video clip, scan the QR code or access via mathsolutions.com/mathworkshop91

Journal Prompts

Your students might already be using reading journals in which they write about their reading, make predictions, summarize, and share whether they like or dislike what they're reading. For a math journal reflection, you could ask students to write to a variety of prompts. Some might include:

- *What mathematical ideas became clear to you? What are you still grappling with?*

- *What learning station did you struggle with today? Why? What station did you feel most successful with and why?*

- *What would you say to someone who missed today's class? How would you summarize the learning that took place?*

- *After meeting in a guided math group, what questions do you still have? What are your big "takeaways?"*

- *Write about a strategy that one of your peers used today. Does this strategy work for any set of numbers? How do you know? How does it compare to a strategy that you used?*

Encourage even your youngest students to write in journals as a reflection. They have amazing ideas that can be expressed using pictures and numbers.

At the end of one of my math classes, Rana's journal entry showed her understanding of different ways to make 6 (see Figure 9–1).

Figure 9–1. Rana's journal entry (*Making 6 is fun. I used my fingers.*)

Turn and Talk

For the turn and talk reflection format, use the same type of prompts used for a journal entry. Instead of writing, ask students to turn and talk with a partner about their responses to the prompt. Give a set time for this. For example, Partner A will have three minutes to talk. Set a timer and let students know when it is Partner B's turn to begin talking. This ensures that one partner does not dominate the conversation and both students have ample time to share their thinking. There may not be time for too much detail, however, the act of verbalizing their reflection and listening to another person's thoughts is an important part of the learning process.

 **VIDEO CLIP 9.2**

Student Reflection: Turn and Talk

In this clip, Ms. Callaway chooses to have fifth graders turn and talk as part of reflection time during math workshop. As you watch this clip, consider the following questions:

- What do you notice about this reflection and how it furthers student understanding?

- What do you notice about this reflection and how it promotes a positive mathematics community in the classroom?

To view this video clip, scan the QR code or access via mathsolutions.com/mathworkshop92

Get Moving

As teachers, we know that having students sit still too long is a recipe for disaster. The get-moving reflection has the added bonus of giving students the opportunity to get up and move. To start this reflection, give students approximately five minutes to write in their journal (if you do not have math journals, having students write on a piece of paper works). Then, rather than a seated turn and talk, invite students to stand up, find a partner, and share what they have written. Here are a couple ways to encourage students to quickly pair up:

- Find a "color" partner—someone wearing the same color as you today.

- Use grouping sticks to make forming groups or pairs a quick and easy process—have every student's name on a popsicle stick and keep them in a jar. Pull out sticks to form groups or partnerships.

Exit Tickets

An exit ticket is a great way to gather information about students' knowledge of mathematics content. To create an exit ticket, display a problem for all students to solve on index cards, or give students different problems (one problem/index card per student) to solve depending on their level. Use what you see on students' exit tickets as a way to guide your instruction or your guided math groups for the next day.

Exit ticket prompts or questions at various grade levels might look like this:

- Rachel checked out 2 books from the library. One book has 32 pages, and the other book has 59 pages. If Rachel reads both books, how many pages will she have read?
- Use the following digits: 1, 3, and 6. What is the largest number you can make? What is the smallest number you can make?
- Write a fraction that is more than $\frac{1}{4}$ and less than $\frac{1}{3}$. Explain how you know.

Four Corners

The four corners reflection encourages students to make a choice and move to one of four labeled corners of the room. It provides a lot of opportunity for creativity. What might this reflection format look like? In the four corners reflection, I label the four corners of my classroom with pictures of kinds of weather: a full sun (corner 1), a partly cloudy sun (corner 2), a rain cloud (corner 3), and a dark grey cloud with a lightning bolt streaking through it (corner 4). I then explain to students that they will use these pictures to communicate how they felt about class today:

- The full sun means you are feeling really strong and positive about your learning today.
- The partly cloudy sun means you had a pretty good day overall, but have a few questions or areas in which you still feel you need practice and support.
- The rain cloud means you're pretty confused about the mathematics.
- The lightning bolt—well—it's been a really rough day.

Ask students to move to the corner that best represents how they're feeling. You might have them focus on a particular part of the day's math workshop. Once students are in their corners, ask them to find a partner and share why they chose the corner they did. Keep an eye out for a student who goes to a corner and doesn't have a partner; join that student. If all corners have more than one person, then join a group and listen in.

You can learn so much about a student and where they are feeling mentally about their day using a reflection like this. During a four corners reflection with a group of first graders once, I noticed that Manav stood up quickly and immediately headed to the lightning bolt. Manav was a boy whom I had been so impressed with throughout the class. He was right on target during the number sense routine, thoughtful in his thinking during learning stations, and really showed a lot of understanding during guided math. I was perplexed as to why he chose the corner he did and purposely went over to listen to his conversation with his partner. Manav passionately shared that he was so upset with himself because he had drawn his 9 "this way" (backward) instead of "this way" (correctly; Manav wrote the number with his fingers in the air). He shared that he had really been trying to remember which way the 9 was supposed to go and he "messed it up again!" My heart broke. Manav couldn't focus on all the great things he accomplished that day because this was weighing so heavily on his shoulders. I was so glad to have heard this explanation, and later, I pulled him aside to encourage him and help him reflect on the good things that happened that day.

While you could use the weather symbols in your classroom for any age, there's no limit to how you might want to label corners. Here are some more of my favorite ways to label the four corners:

- *Effort.* Label the corners 1 to 4 and connect them to a rubric where 4 means students gave their best effort that day, and the 1 means they felt that they did not put effort into the mathematics activities.

- *Perception/Feelings.* Emojis can go a long way in understanding how a student might have perceived and/or felt about their involvement in an activity. Were they bored? (Corner 1 might have a sleeping emoji.) Were they upset? (Corner 2 might have a red-in-the-face frowning emoji.) Were they loving this activity? (Corner 3 might have an emoji with heart-struck eyes.) Do they still have questions or wonderings? (Corner 4 might have an emoji with an inquisitive expression.)

- *Understanding.* Label the four corners with photos of four stages of a flower's growth, from seed to bloom. Students choose the corner that best represents where they feel they are in the understanding of a concept. Corner 1 (a seed) means that they have just started to think about this concept. Corner 2 (a sprout) means that they are emerging with ideas about this topic. Corner 3 (a stalk or flower bud) means that they have developed a pretty good understanding of the concept and are still working on making connections. Corner 4 (a flower in bloom) means that they understand this concept and can explain it to others.

Connecting the Chapter to Your Practice

- How might you ensure that you leave time for a reflection at the end of math workshop? Which of the reflection formats shared in this chapter might allow you to get a lot of information in a short amount of time? Which best meets the age of your students?

- While each day is different, what information are you hoping to collect at the conclusion of math workshop? How can the reflection help you gather that information?

 VIDEO CLIPS 3.1, 4.1, and 5.1, Revisited ················

Rewatch these three clips, paying special attention to the student reflection part of each video and consider the following questions:
- What do you notice happening in each reflection?
- How does the student reflection component of each math workshop structure contribute to the overall effectiveness and success of the structure?

Video Clip 3.1   Video Clip 4.1   Video Clip 5.1

To view these video clips, scan the QR codes or access via mathsolutions.com/mathworkshop31, mathsolutions.com/mathworkshop41, and mathsolutions.com/mathworkshop51

CHAPTER 10 You're Ready, You're Set, Go!

Reviewing the Steps

This chapter attempts to review and tie together everything shared about math workshop from the previous chapters. It is the final "hoorah" for getting you on board with running a smooth and successful math workshop. I recommend you read this chapter after you've familiarized yourself with the previous chapters.

Step 1: Understand Math Workshop

In Chapter 1 you read about why math workshop should be the model of instruction in your classroom and in all classrooms around the world. You know that it promotes a positive learning environment, encourages a growth mindset, and boosts a student's conceptual understanding of mathematics content. Through a math workshop model of instruction, students are encouraged to collaborate and persevere through challenging mathematics. And, best yet, they do all this while having fun with math and truly believing in themselves as mathematicians!

You also learned that a teacher's job is important in math workshop. A teacher makes all the difference in the world. The role of the teacher in math workshop includes facilitating, clarifying, connecting, monitoring, and collecting data as students solve problems.

Your most important shift is your mindset!

Often the biggest shift for us as teachers in starting a math workshop model of instruction is getting over our own dislike or fear of teaching mathematics. Many of us have had poor experiences in mathematics, making the idea of a differentiated, fun mathematics environment seem nearly impossible. I've heard countless teachers over the years say things like, "I'm not a math person!" or "Math is not my thing!" These kinds of statements must not cross our lips if we want to send a positive message to our students about mathematics. We must ensure that all students are in a learning environment with a teacher who believes in them. In turn we must believe in our ability to help move students forward in their mathematical thinking. We also need to ensure that our colleagues are aware of what their negative comments can do to a student's mathematical thinking. This means educating other staff members and the school community.

Step 2: Prepare Your Students for Math Workshop

Chapter 2 addressed the importance of preparing students for this shift in mathematics. In it we learned about the three buckets of math workshop—classroom arrangement, routines and procedures, and mathematics community. These represent the conditions that must be in place to ensure an effective and successful math workshop. Working to fill the three buckets is something that we as teachers need to do prior to beginning math workshop, and it is something that we need to reflect on throughout our journey. As you begin math workshop, make sure you have carefully considered where your classroom, students, and you are now with these three buckets. Revisit the twenty minilessons in Chapter 2 as needed to prepare your students (these lessons can also be revisited throughout math workshop).

Step 3: Decide Your Math Workshop Structure

See Reproducible 14 for an overview of all three math workshop structures.

Chapters 3 through 5 introduced three distinct structures of math workshop: Task and Share; Focus Lesson, Guided Math, and Learning Stations; and Guided Math and Learning Stations (see Reproducible 14 for an overview of all three structures). There may be variations of these structures that you will find effective as you dig deeper into the process of math workshop; but for starters, you'll likely be grappling with the question *Which one of the three structures should I use?* In a nutshell, Figure 10–1 illustrates the thought processes I take in deciding on my math workshop structure.

What task can I use to introduce this unit so that all students have access to the content, I gain an understanding of what students know and don't know yet, and students gain a conceptual understanding of why we would want to learn this?

This results in starting the majority of all units with the Task and Share Structure

Is this new content that students have not been exposed to in the past?

If the answer is YES, choose the Focus Lesson, Guided Math, and Learning Stations structure

If the answer is NO, use the Guided Math and Learning Stations structure

Do I have a new learning station to introduce to my students?

If the answer is YES, then use the Focus Lesson, Guided Math, and Learning Stations structure and use the focus lesson time to ensure everyone knows the station

If the answer is NO, then get right into the Guided Math and Learning Stations structure

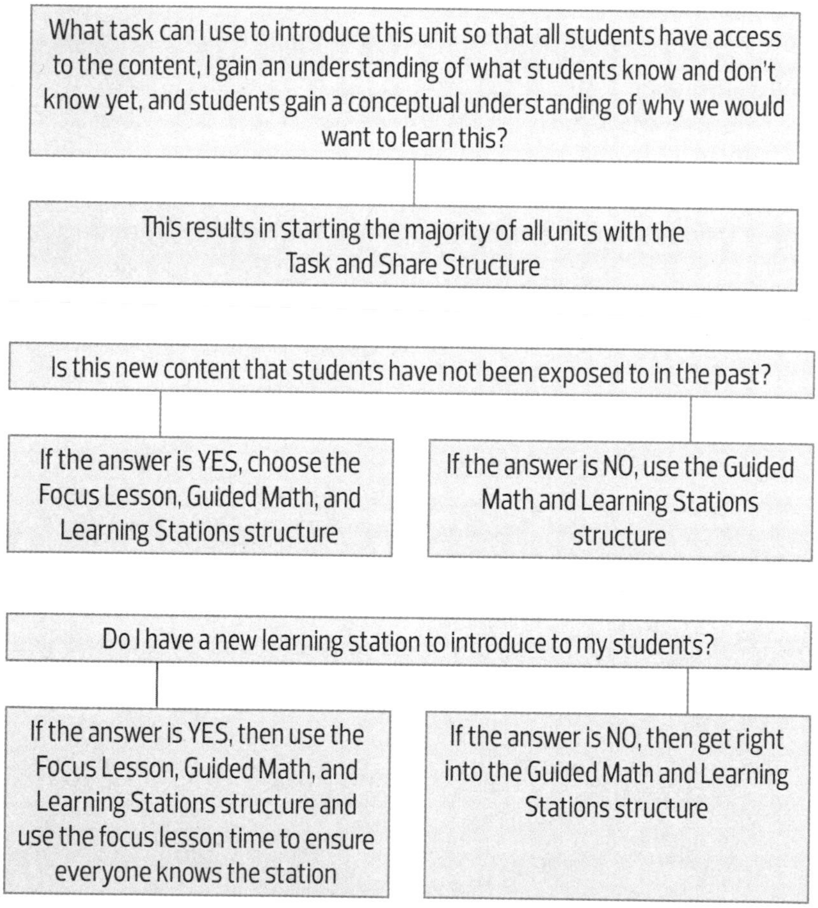

Figure 10–1. Deciding on a math workshop structure

Step 4: Facilitate Your Math Workshop

Chapters 6 through 9 focused on the components found in each of the three structures of math workshop. By focusing on how to efficiently and effectively facilitate number sense routines, learning stations, guided math, and student reflections, your confidence in putting these together in a full math class will grow.

It's important to remember that the components of the three math workshop structures can be used in different places. For example, you might choose to take the task component found in the Task and Share structure and do it in a guided math group as part of the Guided Math and Learning Stations structure. As you start to see how math workshop is a fluid, ever-changing model, you may find yourself grappling with more questions. A common question teachers have as they become more familiar with the components of math workshop is: *How do I choose what to teach in a whole-group focus lesson and what to save for my guided math groups?*

As we've learned in Chapter 8, guided math is a time that you are teaching to either a small group of students or having an individual conference. In either case, the focus lesson is not absent, it is just done with a few students rather than with the whole class. By utilizing small-group and one-on-one opportunities, you can observe and question students in ways that you can't when teaching the whole group.

There are times when important conversations need to happen with the whole group with you acting as facilitator and helping students make connections. For example, if I am a fourth-grade teacher, and I'm planning for an upcoming unit about decimals, I will definitely allow for more days spent with the Focus Lesson, Guided Math, and Learning Stations structure since this will be the first exposure to decimals for my students. On the other hand, if I'm a second-grade teacher planning for an upcoming unit about shapes, I know that my students have been exposed to shapes since kindergarten. I will find out who remembers what about shapes either with a brief individual or small-group interview and then move on to the Guided Math and Learning Stations structure.

Of course, we all have students who are new to the school, district, state, or country and do not have the same exposure as other students. As teachers we shouldn't attempt to fill their gaps in understanding in front of the whole class. Guided math groups and individual conferencing more appropriately allow us to focus on what these students need in order to move them along in their understanding and reasoning.

Last but not least, knowing your standards and the standards that your students were previously exposed to will be of significant help in deciding when to do a focus lesson as a whole group and when to lean on small groups and/or individual conferencing for such.

Math workshop is your orchestra!

You know the why, you know the what, and you know the how. It's now time to put all of this into practice. In math workshop you are ensuring that all the components are running smoothly, are engaging and accessible, and are mathematically rich.

What exactly you do will change depending on the math workshop structure you use and the component on which you are working. Two components of math workshop, the number sense routine and student reflection, occur each and every day in math workshop, regardless of which structure you choose to implement that day. Therefore, it will likely be important to "change up the music" and ensure your students are exposed to a variety of number sense routines and reflections so they don't become bored and "tune out." Some components, like the focus lesson and learning stations, occur in only two of the structures: (1) Focus Lesson, Guided Math, and Learning Stations and (2) Guided Math and Learning Stations. On the other hand, the Task and Share structure has components that these structures do not. In the end, whatever the components may be and however you choose to use them, when in harmony, they will lead to a beautifully crafted mathematics lesson.

Your Getting Started Checklist

Okay, you're ready . . . but maybe you want to check your readiness . . . just how ready are you? Reproducible 15 offers a checklist that will help you to determine what you already have in place that supports math workshop. It will also help to identify things you need to establish so that math workshop can run effectively and efficiently.

See Reproducible I5, *Getting Started Checklist.*

Getting Started Checklist

Use this checklist to help you determine what you already have in place that would support math workshop. It will also help to identify steps you may need to take so that math workshop can run effectively and efficiently.

DO I HAVE . . .	YES/NO	NOTES
an anchor chart (created as a class) that identifies expectations for students during math workshop?		
students who are willing to share with one another without fear of making mistakes?		
a place for the whole-group number sense routine?		
a place to pull small groups of students for guided math?		
fluid groups of students for guided math?		
a place for learning stations and the corresponding materials?		
resources to create learning stations?		
an organizational system, such as menus, that effectively communicates the learning station options to students?		
a place to share and reflect as a whole group?		
an anecdotal record system?		

Steps I need to take to better prepare for math workshop:

Reproducible 15. Getting Started Checklist

Go Slow to Go Fast!

So, you went through your list and you checked it twice. You are ready to go. Great! I can't tell you how excited I am for you to begin math workshop. I get excited for the students in your classroom too; math workshop is going to make a huge difference in their attitude toward and understanding of mathematics.

Once you get started, you will never want to go back. You will know your students' strengths and struggles more than ever. You will see a renewed energy and enthusiasm in your students, and you will begin to like mathematics even if it has been your worst nemesis in the past. Still, I urge you to *Go Slow to Go Fast!* Your first month of math workshop does not need to look like the classrooms filmed for the videos in this book. In fact, the first few days might be downright difficult. Just remember that you are not alone. I have experienced challenges along with the thousands of teachers who have also tried math workshop. But don't let setbacks stop you. Push forward. Stay focused. And, when you hit a roadblock, turn to this resource for guidance and reinforcement. You can do it!

I've chosen to conclude this chapter with a lesson that resonates with what to keep in mind in your first few days of math workshop.

 VIDEO CLIP 10.1 ·

Go Slow to Go Fast!

In this clip, the author Ms. Lempp advises teachers starting math workshop to "go slow to go fast." As you watch this clip, consider the following questions:

- How do you feel about the mantra, "Go slow to go fast"?
- Have you experienced a situation in which too many changes at once caused you or your colleagues to give up? How do you think the situation could've been handled differently?

To view this video clip, scan the QR code or access via mathsolutions.com/mathworkshop101

· ·

WHAT THE TEACHER DOES . . .	WHAT THE STUDENTS DO . . .
The teacher starts each day with a number sense routine.	Students think about the following and share their ideas. *Which One Doesn't Belong?* 
The teacher facilitates a short focus lesson that consists of an open–ended problem (one with multiple acceptable answers). The teacher refrains from telling too much and coming to students' rescue; this is not a time to model your way.	In small groups, students solve the following problem: *Julio, Ramon, and Simon together have 24 tokens for the arcade. How many tokens might each boy have?*
The teacher records students' ideas where everyone can see them and prompts other students' thinking: • *Do you agree or disagree with _____'s answer?* • *Did anyone else think of it differently?* • *Turn and talk to your partner about why _____'s numbers work and how the answer compares to your answer.* The teacher concentrates on making focus lesson time heavy on student talk and light on teacher talk.	Students come back together as a whole class and share some of the ways in which they solved the problem.
The teacher monitors students working in small groups and asks questions like: • *Did you get all the possible combinations?* • *How do you know?*	Once students realize that there are several correct answers to the problem, they return to their small groups to determine as many answers as possible.
The teacher provides students with a learning station activity to work on with a partner. The teacher reinforces learning station expectations, including how students collaborate with partners, how to treat the materials, and how to maintain conversations around the mathematics.	Students acquaint themselves with the learning station activity: *Matching Game* 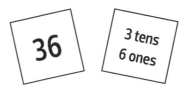

(continued)

WHAT THE TEACHER DOES . . .	WHAT THE STUDENTS DO . . .
The teacher monitors students as they work. This includes providing feedback and looking and listening for how students are talking to one another. Are they being respectful? Are they sharing in the responsibility or is one partner dominating? Are they using quiet voices that are suitable for the classroom? Are they remaining on task the entire time? Finally, did they clean up their materials?	Students engage in the activity. 
The teacher closes with a reflection.	The students reflect on their learning by completing the following exit ticket prompt: *Nathan and Sam ran a total of 17 miles. How many miles might each boy have run?*

Remember, *Go Slow to Go Fast*. In the beginning phase of implementing math workshop, you do not need to jump into guided math groups or have several options for learning stations. Instead take the necessary time to ensure that students are able to work respectfully with one another and take risks. Continually circulate and offer feedback on how students are working. With patience, persistence, and enthusiasm, I assure you your math workshop will only get better and better.

Connecting the Chapter to Your Practice

- What is your story as a student of mathematics and how might that impact your teaching of mathematics?
- What are you most excited about in starting a math workshop model of instruction?
- What is one concern you may have about starting a math workshop model of instruction? What resources are available to you that could help you with this concern?

Reflect on and Refine Your Math Workshop

STEP 5

In this section, you'll find additional support critical to your use of math workshop. I like to think of these chapters as your own personal "instructional coach." When in doubt, turn to these chapters to think about things differently or find answers to your questions. You'll likely return to these chapters time and time again as you progress in making math workshop your own. Chapter 11 has reflective questions to consider whether you are implementing math workshop solo, with a team, or as a whole school. You will also find suggested action steps to choose from, especially when you are feeling stuck or unsure of where to go next. Chapter 12 is in the form of Frequently Asked Questions (FAQs). These were collected from my own experiences and the experiences of other teachers who have made a commitment to teach using math workshop.

· ·

Chapters in Step 5

Reflecting on Implementation

Chapter 11

VIDEO CLIP 10.1, Revisited · · · · · · · · · · · · · · · · · ·

Go Slow to Go Fast!, Revisited

In this clip, the author Ms. Lempp emphasizes the importance of taking one step at a time when implementing math workshop—and remembering to reflect as you go. As you watch the clip, consider the following question:

• What ways do you reflect as an educator?

To view this video clip, scan the QR code or access via mathsolutions.com/mathworkshop101

Ways to Reflect as Educators

In Chapter 9 we looked at the importance of student reflection as a component of math workshop. It's equally important for us as teachers to spend time reflecting. Reflecting on our work provides us with the opportunity to identify the strengths and struggles of the lessons we have planned. Reflection helps us look inward at the choices we've made for students. During a year with a particularly challenging group of students, I realized that I needed to ask myself more "I" questions. If I expected or hoped for something to be different in my classroom, I needed to look at what I could do as the teacher to change things for the better.

I'm aware that planning mathematics is probably not the only subject area on your mind. You have other content areas to consider, as well as grading, parent conferences, committees on which you serve, and (gasp) a social or personal life. However, taking the time to independently reflect following a day of math workshop—and reflect with your colleagues—is a sure way to make your mathematics instruction stronger. Following are ways I've found helpful to reflect on my implementation of math workshop.

> Reflection is deliberate and structured thinking about choices. It is an integral step to improving our practice. Through reflection, we as educators can look clearly at our successes and struggles and consider options for change.
>
> —Taryn Sanders, quoted in the "Importance of Reflection"

Reflect on the Data

As teachers we collect a variety of data before, during, and at the end of our lessons. This data might be in the form of an observation, a piece of student work, or a test. This data informs our instruction and supports us in continually learning more about our students. Part of reflecting is dissagregating the data in order to determine if it says what we anticipated it saying. Then we must take action accordingly. I've found that there are three main forms of data that drive my instructional practices and support me in reflecting:

- Formative Data
- Summative Data
- Social Data

The word *data* may make you cringe; we've all likely felt inundated with it and felt that summative data takes priority or that we have to test students too much when all we really want to do is spend time on instruction. I find it helpful to think of data as information. We use all of the information we gather to plan for the next great lesson. This cycle continues day after day.

Formative Data Formative data is associated with assessment *for* learning. Formative assessment takes place on a daily basis, as teachers are constantly on the lookout for students' demonstration of knowledge. This type of data can be collected from various forms of assessment including exit cards, checklists, anecdotal records from previous lessons, and observation. Another purpose for formative data is to provide feedback to students and monitor student progress.

Summative Data In contrast, summative data is associated with assessment *of* learning. While summative data can also support decision making in the classroom, these assessments most often happen after learning occurs. Summative assessments could be in the form of unit tests or state test results. While all summative data can be used in a formative way, not all formative data is summative.

Social Data Social data is just as important, and could fit in the category of formative data, because this is also data observed over time. Social data is the information that we collect about students' preferences, learning styles, and interests. When we are in tune with our students, we have a better idea of who can and can't work well together, who can show their thinking the best using manipulatives, who has a fear or dislike of mathematics, and so on.

Ask Yourself Reflective Questions

We can ask ourselves reflective questions privately or with colleagues during team planning. If your role is administrator or coach, reflective questions can be used to promote conversations with teachers.

This resource has offered reflective questions (Connecting the Chapter to Your Practice) at the end of each chapter. Figure 11–1 shows a few more reflective questions as well as actions steps to consider when faced with a dilemma.

REFLECTIVE QUESTION	ACTION STEPS
Does the data match my predictions about students' prior knowledge of the content?	Refer to the standards. Plan interview questions for a few students to determine gaps or holes in their understanding. Conduct interviews during guided math time to inform future instruction.
What content might I want to spend more time on with students?	If the whole class needs more instruction on the content, plan a focus lesson. If only some students need more instruction on the content, plan a guided math lesson for those students.
Who is ready to move on? Who needs more time? Have I encountered any surprises in the way I've chosen to group students?	Use pre-assessments, checklists, anecdotal records, and other student work samples to determine student progress on a standard. Plan focus lessons, guided groups, and learning station activities that will help meet students' needs.
What does the data tell me about my own practice as an instructor? What worked? What didn't work?	Consider making changes to: • how students are grouped, • how opportunities are provided for students to talk about the math, • the questions being asked to students, and • the learning stations.
How could my organizational system be improved?	Consider: • revisiting routines and procedures that relate to an area of concern, • going into greater detail about how students know what choices they have during stations or what to do when they are finished, and • revising partners or small groups.

Figure 11–1. Additional reflective questions

REFLECTIVE QUESTION	ACTION STEPS
Is classroom management standing in my way of continuing with math workshop?	Clarify expectations with students. Revisit the anchor chart made during the first twenty days (see the minilessons in Chapter 2).
	Have a ten-minute class meeting where students practice the expectations and discuss them.
	Set a goal with students to provide intentional feedback for one week. Carry through with the goal in hopes of getting students back on track.
	Use one of the reflection times at the end of a day of math workshop to reflect on areas of concern rather than the math content in order to gather more information from students.
How did the lesson go? What does it mean for tomorrow? Do I need to adapt the lesson the next time I teach it?	Make notes about how to modify the lesson for the next time it's taught.
	Use anecdotal records from guided math, work samples from learning stations, and exit tickets or reflections to make decisions.

Figure 11–1. *(Continued)*

When first starting off, do not feel as though all the action steps listed in Figure 11–1 need to occur simultaneously. Focus on one of the action items at a time until it becomes a habit of mind.

Prior to moving forward, be sure that you have considered the current reality of the math workshop model in your classroom. Taking time to reflect will help you identify what can be refined and improved so your math workshop runs more effectively and efficiently each and every day.

Chapter 12 Refining Your Practice—FAQs

 **VIDEO CLIP 12.1** ·····················

Overcoming Roadblocks

Trying something new doesn't come without roadblocks. In this clip, author Ms. Lempp shares two such roadblocks that teachers might encounter in math workshop, and advises how to deal with them. As you watch this clip, consider the following question:

- What roadblocks might you be concerned about as you make math workshop a part of your classroom?

To view this video clip, scan the QR code or access via mathsolutions.com/mathworkshop121

··

The Art of Refinement

As teachers, we are constantly trying to refine our work. Trying something new doesn't come without roadblocks, and time is often the greatest of these barriers. Some of you reading this book may work in a school with instructional coaches and resource teachers who are there to help you brainstorm about curriculum or pedagogy questions. Some of you may have a strong team with whom you can collaborate to work through concerns. And some of you charge through your work solo. In any of these instances, it's my hope that this final chapter might be a bit like a coach, teammate, or sounding board for you.

Whereas many questions are asked and answered throughout this book, specific to each component of math workshop, this final chapter answers questions I've had and received from others about math workshop regardless of the structure you implement or where you are in your journey. This section is in a question-and-answer format to help you easily access the information. These questions are not meant to overwhelm you or hold you back from math workshop—rather they are meant to help you refine your practice and continue forward.

I Believe in Math Workshop, But How Can I Do It This Year with Such a Challenging Group of Kids?

Having a "challenging group of kids" is a perfect reason why you *should* do math workshop! One of the first groups of students with whom I used math workshop (and way before I called it math workshop) was a class of sixth graders who called themselves the "ghetto class." How awful! These students had no faith in themselves as students, much less as mathematicians. They felt as though school had failed them, and their failing grades over the last several years showed that they gave up. It was sad. In this class, eight of the students had an Individual Education Plan and the majority of them were considered economically disadvantaged. It was clear that this group needed something very different from the traditional model of instruction.

And no surprise—they thrived in a math workshop model of instruction. Their needs were met through differentiated small-group instruction. They were respected as individuals and seen as contributors in the classroom. These were students for whom the traditional algorithms that they had been attempting to memorize and keep track of in their head just never made sense. Being allowed the freedom of student-invented strategies and academic discourse, this amazing group of students started to understand math as a process rather than a system of right or wrong answers. Bottom line: don't let a challenging class or student dissuade you from doing math workshop—rather, math workshop just may be the answer!

Why Does Math Workshop Seem Like a Lot More Work Than I Was Doing Before?

Change is hard. And, in the beginning, anything that is worthwhile will take work. However, soon your work will pay off and you will even find that math workshop is easier on you than the demands of a traditional classroom. You will no longer waste time planning lessons that don't meet many students where they are—and end up increasing their confusion. You won't have to plan intervention. Instead, the math workshop lessons you plan will be "just right" for students. Math workshop allows time for "spiraling" the big ideas throughout the year, which also gives students more time to practice and to process.

What Happens When My Students Go to Middle School and Their Math Class Looks Entirely Different?

Math instruction at the middle school level doesn't have to look that different. I used math workshop when I taught in a middle school, and I saw great success. Middle school students benefit from all the same things that elementary school students do, including discourse, the use of manipulatives, exploration, and problem solving. So don't change your way so that students are prepared for traditional instruction later. Instead, have the positive presupposition that mathematics instruction is going to improve everywhere—including in middle and high school.

My Students Just Won't Talk About Math During Workshop. How Do I Get Them to Share Ideas?

There is nothing worse for a teacher who really, really wants her students to engage in rich conversations about mathematics only to hear silence. When I hear silence in mathematics, I often think that there are two reasons for such: students assume they're wrong and/or I really haven't given them something that encourages discussion. Let's explore each of these reasons in more detail.

Students assume they're wrong I've witnessed so many students look completely baffled when the teacher asks them to explain "how they know." Most of these students, instead of explaining, assume that they must be wrong, and immediately change their answer. Discussion about mathematics has not yet become their norm. If this happens in your classroom, don't worry. Your students will get there. They will get there because you know the value of discussion. Continue to work on developing a mathematical community in your classroom where students can freely take risks, ask questions, and share ideas (remember the twenty minilessons in Chapter 2).

The task doesn't encourage discussion Sometimes students aren't talking because there is very little to discuss. When presented with a closed task, students rarely have much to share because there is only one answer and one way to solve the problem. If you are staring out on a sea of quiet students, you might want to look at the activity in which they are involved. Can you make it more open-ended? See Figure 12–1 on the next page for examples of transforming a closed task into an open-ended one.

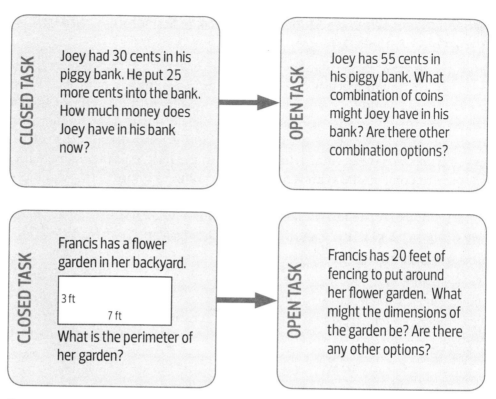

Figure 12–1. How can you transform a closed task to an open-ended task?

The Math Workshop Structures in This Resource Are Created for a Sixty-Minute Math Class. What If I Have More Time? Less Time?

Math workshop, because it is more about the philosophy of how students learn and process number ideas, can be used no matter how much time you have. I'm a believer that the more time you have for math, the better. Having more time will mean that you get to do more like meet with more guided math groups. Having less time will mean that you get to fewer groups, and you have to really be a stickler about not going over fifteen minutes for your focus lesson.

What If I Have One Student Who Needs Something Entirely Different from Everyone Else?

It's all about differentiation! As teachers we understand that textbooks do not drive our mathematical goals; our state standards and our students' needs drive instruction. Regardless of the resources that have been chosen by our school or school district, we should make an effort to understand our standards inside and out: what the standards are for this school year, the standards students have been instructed under in the past, and the mathematics that are to come in the years ahead.

Using this information, we are better able to support a student's gap in understanding, related to the standard being taught. In addition, we are able to clearly see if a student is already showing mastery of that said standard and what related standards they will be faced with in the future. Being able to fluidly move on grade level, below grade level, and above grade level allows us to support students when they need something specific.

But What About the Tests?

Tests! I know we all have them, and I'm betting we can all relate to the stress that comes with them. However, remember that math workshop will make your core instruction stronger. Students will get more out of their math time with you. Mathematics will be more meaningful, and students will more naturally transform into mathematical thinkers and problem solvers. So, bring the test on! It won't matter what the test looks like; with true conceptual understanding, use of strategies and the know-how to problem-solve, students will do just fine on any test that comes their way.

A Final Note

Being intentional before, during, and after math workshop will help make it run as effectively and efficiently as possible. Students will be engaged like never before. Student confidence and perseverance will increase, motivation will soar, and you will start to see each and every student exhibit a growth mindset. Using math workshop will help students see themselves as mathematicians, thinkers, and problem solvers. Isn't that exactly what we want for our students?

If you do not find an answer to your question in this book, I trust that the answer is within you or a member of your team. Talk openly with one another about your transition to math workshop. Celebrate with one another as you make it over each hurdle and as you witness your students become amazing problem solvers. Be there to support one another when the transition isn't going as well. Remember all the beneficial reasons why you started math workshop in the first place, and remember that you are not alone.

Also, remember to give yourself a break. I believe you are a great teacher already. I know this because you just spent your own time reading a book about how to make math even better for your students. You have little free time, and I acknowledge and respect that. I appreciate you and all the work you are already doing to make sure that your students have a love of learning, feel supported, and realize their full potential. I wish you the best of success in your math workshop journey; I believe in you and I know you can do this!

References

Bresser, R., and C. Holtzman. 2006. *Minilessons for Math Practice, Grades K–2*. Sausalito, CA: Math Solutions.

Bresser, R., K. Melanese, and C. Sphar. 2006. *Minilessons for Math Practice, Grades 3–5*. Sausalito, CA: Math Solutions.

———. 2009. *Supporting English Language Learners in Math Class, Grades K–2*. Sausalito, CA: Math Solutions.

———. 2009. *Supporting English Language Learners in Math Class, Grades 3–5*. Sausalito, CA: Math Solutions.

Buffum, A., M. Mattos, and C. Weber. 2009. *Pyramid Response to Intervention: RTI, Professional Learning Communities, and How to Respond When Kids Don't Learn*. Bloomington, IN: Solution Tree.

———. 2012. *Simplifying Response to Intervention: Four Essential Guiding Principles*. Bloomington, IN: Solution Tree.

Burns, M. 1996. *50 Problem-Solving Lessons, Grades 1–6: The Best from 10 Years of Math Solutions Newsletters*. Sausalito, CA: Math Solutions.

———. 2015. *About Teaching Mathematics*. 4th ed. Sausalito, CA: Math Solutions.

Bushey, G., and J. Moser. 2014. *The Daily 5: Fostering Literacy Independence in the Elementary Grades*. Portland, ME: Stenhouse.

Carpenter, T. P., E. Fennema, M. Loef Franke, L. Levi, and S. B. Empson. 1999. *Children's Mathematics: Cognitively Guided Instruction*. Portsmouth, NH: Heinemann.

Chapin, S. H., O'Connor, C., and N. Canavan Anderson. 2013. *Talk Moves: A Teacher's Guide to Using Classroom Discussions in Math*. 3d ed. Sausalito, CA: Math Solutions.

Collins, A. M. 2012. *50 Leveled Math Problems: Level 5*. Huntington Beach, CA: Shell.

———. 2012. *50 Leveled Math Problems: Level 6*. Huntington Beach, CA: Shell.

Dacey, L. 2012. *50 Leveled Math Problems: Level 1*. Huntington Beach, CA: Shell.

———. 2012. *50 Leveled Math Problems: Level 2*. Huntington Beach, CA: Shell.

———. 2012. *50 Leveled Math Problems: Level 3*. Huntington Beach, CA: Shell.

————. 2012. *50 Leveled Math Problems: Level 4*. Huntington Beach, CA: Shell.

Dacey, L., J. Bamford Lynch, and R. Eston Salemi. 2013. *How to Differentiate Your Instruction, Grades K–6*. Sausalito, CA: Math Solutions.

Diller, D. 2011. *Math Work Stations: Independent Learning You Can Count On, K–2*. Portland, ME: Stenhouse.

DuFour, R., and R. Eaker. 1998. *Professional Learning Communities at Work: Best Practices for Enhancing Student Achievement*. Bloomington, IN: Solution Tree.

Fountas, I., and G. S. Pinnell. 2001. *Guiding Readers and Writers (Grades 3–6): Teaching Comprehension, Genre, and Content Literacy*. Portsmouth, NH: Heinemann.

Guthrie, J. T., A. Wigfield, and K. Perencevich. 2004. "Scaffolding for Motivation and Engagement in Reading." In *Motivating Reading Comprehension: Content-Oriented Reading Instruction*, eds. John T. Guthrie, Allan Wigfield, and Katherine C. Perencevich, 55–86. Mahwah, NJ: Erlbaum.

Hattie, J. 2009. *Visible Learning: A Synthesis of Over 800 Meta-Analyses Relating to Achievement*. New York: Routledge.

Jackson, K. J., E. C. Shahan, L. K. Gibbons, and P. A. Cobb. 2012. "Launching Complex Tasks." *Mathematics Teaching in the Middle School* 18(1): 24–29.

Jensen, E. 2003. *Tools for Engagement: Managing Emotional States for Learner Success*. San Diego, CA: The Brain Store.

Melanese, K., L. Chung, and C. Forbes. 2011. *Supporting English Language Learners in Math Class, Grades 6–8*. Sausalito, CA: Math Solutions.

Parrish, S. 2010, 2014. *Number Talks: Whole Number Computation*. Sausalito, CA: Math Solutions.

Parrish, S., and A. Dominick. 2016. *Number Talks: Fractions, Decimals, and Percentages*. Sausalito, CA: Math Solutions.

Patall, E. A., H. Cooper, and J. C. Robinson. 2008. "The Effects of Choice on Intrinsic Motivation and Related Outcomes: A Meta-Analysis of Research Findings." *Psychology Bulletin* 134(2): 270–300.

Petersen, J. 2013. *Math Games for Number and Operations and Algebraic Thinking: Games to Support Independent Practice in Math Workshops and More, Grades K–5*. Sausalito, CA: Math Solutions.

Reinhart, S. C. 2000. "Never Say Anything a Kid Can Say." *Mathematics Teaching in the Middle School* 5(8).

Sanders, T. n.d. "The Importance of Reflection." United Federation of Teachers. www.uft.org/teaching/pip-importance-reflection

Schuster, L., and N. Canavan Anderson. 2005. *Good Questions for Math Teaching: Why Ask Them and What to Ask, Grades 5–8.* Sausalito, CA: Math Solutions.

Seeley, C. 2009. *Faster Isn't Smarter.* Sausalito, CA: Math Solutions.

———. 2014. *Smarter Than We Think.* Sausalito, CA: Math Solutions.

———. 2015. *Faster Isn't Smarter.* 2d ed. Sausalito, CA: Math Solutions.

Shumway, J. 2011. *Number Sense Routines: Building Numerical Literacy Every Day in Grades K–3.* Portland, ME: Stenhouse.

Siena, M. 2009. *From Reading to Math: How Best Practices in Literacy Can Make You a Better Math Teacher.* Sausalito, CA: Math Solutions.

Smith, M. S., and M. K. Stein. 2011. *5 Practices for Orchestrating Effective Mathematics Discussions.* Reston, VA: National Council of Teachers of Mathematics.

Sullivan, P., and P. Lilburn. 2002. *Good Questions for Math Teaching, Grades K–6: Why Ask Them and What to Ask.* Sausalito, CA: Math Solutions.

Tomlinson, C. A., and M. B. Imbeau. 2010. *Leading and Managing a Differentiated Classroom.* Alexandria, VA: ASCD.

Van de Walle, J. A., K. S. Karp, and J. M. Bay-Williams. 2012. *Elementary and Middle School Mathematics: Teaching Developmentally.* 8th ed. Boston: Pearson.

Zwiers, J., and M. Crawford. 2011. *Academic Conversations: Classroom Talk That Fosters Critical Thinking and Content Understanding.* Portland, ME: Stenhouse.